Air Fryer All Day

Air Fryer All Day

120
TRIED-AND-TRUE RECIPES FOR FAMILY-FRIENDLY COMFORT FOOD

Rebecca Abbott and Jennifer West

CO-FOUNDERS OF Air Frying Foodie

WITH Rachel Holtzman

HARVEST
An Imprint of WILLIAM MORROW

*To Mark. Thank you for all of your support and
encouragement, endless dish-washing, late-night trips
to the grocery store, taste-testing, and prayers,
and for dreaming with us.
And to our amazing kids: Grant, Ryan, Jade,
Taylor, Avery, and Addison*

Contents

Introduction

On January 26, 2022, the two of us sat at a table in a local restaurant surrounded by friends, family, and raised glasses of Champagne. Because on that day, we'd hit the mother of all trifectas: one million followers on our Facebook group, one million page views on our website, and a feature in the *New York Times*. (Not exactly just another Wednesday, at least not in our worlds!) And because there just happens to be 1,200 miles that lie between our hometowns, we did the whole thing over FaceTime—the norm for our long-distance friendship turned sisterhood turned business partnership, which bounces between text, Messenger, and Marco Polo all day, every day. Sometimes all at once.

If you had told us *just one year before* that we'd be running the number one air frying–dedicated Facebook group and the destination website for air frying recipes, we'd have said you were nuts. But then again, neither of us was expecting to take an online food photography course because of a worldwide pandemic shutting down just about everything else, and we sure as heck weren't expecting to make a lifelong friend who happens to live across the country. And being the type A, OCD, twenty-mental-tabs-running-at-once kind of gals that we are, it really was just a matter of time before we started to dream big. Or at least big enough to fit in a 6-quart air fryer basket.

After buying an air fryer in 2019 to develop recipes for a client's blog, Rebecca started out making what most people assume the appliance is for: fried finger foods, jumbo batches of one-note crispy things, and in her spare time, heating up leftovers. But as a culinary instructor and an avid baker, she couldn't help but wonder what else she might be able to whip up. When an expertly set, perfectly creamy cheesecake emerged from her air fryer after a bit of fine-tuning of her recipe, she knew that this was much more than just a passing kitchen fad.

Meanwhile, in November 2020, Jen had launched a Facebook group called Easy Air Fryer Recipes. At first, we were the only two subscribers on the site, plus about eight other friends. A few days later, there were one hundred of us. By the following week, there were one thousand. When the group hit fifteen thousand subscribers in a matter of weeks with no sign of slowing down, we realized that we had found our next big adventure: Air Frying Foodie was born.

Since launching this community, we've had two goals that drive everything we do: Our recipes need to be iron-clad dependable and delectable, and we need to give our followers what they want—delicious, cooked-from-scratch meals in less than 30 minutes using a handful of unfussy ingredients. The result is something really special—every day we get to help millions of people spend less time worrying about what's for breakfast, lunch, or dinner. Believe us—we've raised kids and know what it's like to walk in from work only to face a tableful of hungry children . . . and then to have to do all the dishes after dinner. We also know what families want. In fact, our kids and grandkids are our regular taste testers. Jen's eleven-year-old daughter, Addy, is one of our best critics, and Rebecca's four-year-old grandson, Lucas, even has his own 2-quart Dash Air Fryer that he loves using to make his own lunches.

We've moved beyond the novelty of using air fryers to reheat frozen taquitos and fry up store-bought ravioli. But the recipes out there haven't caught up! That's why we wanted to give you a dependable rotation of heartfelt, comfort food dishes your entire family will enjoy in a fraction of the time and hold your hand while you make them. As an added bonus, you will use less oil than you would when cooking on the stove top or in the oven and have very few dishes to wash afterward. That's what *Air Fryer All Day* is about.

The 125 recipes you'll find here are what we know you've been waiting for: foolproof, feel-good meals using ingredients that you're already bringing home from the store and that you can feel confident your family will enjoy. From Spinach and Feta Egg Bites, Strawberry Scones, and Chicken and Waffle Scramble for breakfast, to Grilled Tomato and Mozzarella Sandwiches and Stuffed Eggplant for lunch, to Fish Tacos, Spicy Beef Stir-Fry, Spaghetti Squash Marinara, Balsamic and Goat Cheese Pizza, and Classic Lasagna for dinner, we've got your entire day covered.

Want to finally master a whole-cooked chicken? We've got a Whole Stuffed Chicken for you.

Perfectly cooked steak? We've got Rib Eye and Asparagus.

Something a little fancy? Lobster Mac 'n' Cheese. (Although we'd argue that you don't need to wait for a special occasion to break that one out!)

Love casseroles as much as we do? There's an entire chapter for that! Complete with assured whole-family hits, such as Enchilada Quinoa Casserole, Beef and Bean Taco Casserole, and Harvest Casserole with Apples, Sausage, and Sweet Potatoes. While these recipes can fully stand on their own as complete meals, we've also included some of our favorite sides, such as Parmesan Brussels Sprouts, Sweet Potato Casserole, and Scalloped Red Potatoes. And we couldn't possibly publish a cookbook without including our signature no-fail desserts, such as Deep-Dish Brownies, Crème Brûlée, and Oatmeal-Raisin Cookies. A majority of these recipes will be brand new to our followers, but we also couldn't resist throwing in a few of the biggest hits that still receive tens of thousands of shares and likes, such as Country-Style Ribs, Chicken Wings, and Cornish Game Hens.

In addition to our recipes, we'll provide the kind of guidance and support that we're known for. We'll kick off the book by answering some of the most frequent questions we get, such as: *Which air fryer is right for me? How do I use the darn thing?* And *What kind of oil should I use?* We get that using an air fryer may be completely new territory for many of you, and for that reason, we want to make sure that you feel as comfortable as possible putting it to work. After all, these recipes will have you covered for breakfast, lunch, dinner, and pretty much everything in between. We'll also talk about general guidelines for cook times and temps so that you can learn how to cook the ingredients you already have in your fridge or freezer or so you can feel confident about picking up whatever looks good at the store (or is on sale). We get that you may be here for our recipes, but we want you to feel comfortable enough to experiment, too.

Ultimately, *Air Fryer All Day* is about doing all the hard work for you—and letting you reap the sweet (and savory) rewards. You can trust that these recipes have been through the type A gauntlet—they've been tested (and tested and tested) until they're absolutely perfect so that all you need to do is grab the ingredients and follow the steps. But more than anything, we want to give you the tools—and a hearty serving of peace of mind—to make satisfying, healthier meals as efficiently and simply as possible. With the help of our recipes and know-how, plus the genius magic that is the air fryer, we're confident that we can give you back the precious time you'd be spending on cooking and doing the dishes so that you can use it to do what matters most—live your life!

How to Use
This Cookbook

1

Whether you've been an air fryer devotee for years or are brand new to using the device, we wanted to make sure that you have all the tools you need to make these recipes as successfully as possible. Luckily, when it comes to air frying, nothing is ever too complicated (a big reason why we love them!). In this section, we'll cover everything from how to choose the right air fryer for you, to fine-tuning our recipes' cook times depending on how your home air fryer cooks, to our favorite tips and tricks. After spending a few minutes here, you should feel ready to tackle your next Chicken Parmesan (page 120) or Deep-Dish Brownies (page 219).

Choosing an Air Fryer

There are SO many air fryers out there, and it can be really confusing to know what to look for—especially if you've never used one before. The good news is that there are a number of great, dependable versions with a wide range of size, price, and capability options. And that selection is only getting bigger and better as more and more people learn about the wonder that is air frying. Because the air fryer market is constantly growing and evolving, we can't give you advice about specific models—as much as we'd love to! Instead, we can give you some guidelines for how you can find the right choice for you and your family.

The best place to start is to ask yourself:

- How much counter space do I have for an air fryer?
- What functions will I be using on my air fryer (i.e., roast, bake, toast, dehydrate, etc.)?
- What is my budget?
- How many people will I regularly want to feed?

Main Categories of Air Fryers

1- TO 4-QUART: These might be small, but they can get the job done. In addition to being a good compact choice for those tighter on space, they're also great for making side dishes. However, if you're feeding fewer than four people, you could also make an entire meal. These models can sometimes have a lower wattage, so be sure to run a Toast Test in your air fryer (opposite) and adjust your cook times accordingly when using our recipes.

5.8- TO 10-QUART: Air fryers in this size range are recommended for feeding a family of 4 to 6 people. The larger basket may allow for simultaneous cooking of two dishes at once or larger recipes. These models may require more cook time due to the additional space and/or food in the air fryer.

26-QUART: To put it into context, these models are large enough to fit a full-size 12- to 15-pound turkey(!). That means that they're perfect for feeding a large family. It's certainly a bigger machine; air fryers of this size are essentially an all-in-one kitchen appliance and are sometimes even used to replace a conventional oven.

BUILT-IN OVEN: This is a great option for those of you who are upgrading your kitchen appliances and are looking to add the air fryer function to your new stove. As you might imagine, this size will accommodate multiple dishes at one time. However, that much cooking space does require more cooking time. It's also worth pointing out that cleanup can be more involved due to splattering. For this reason, we love using our oven feature for baking and saving our messier, saucier recipes for the smaller basket-style models.

MULTIFUNCTION (6-IN-1, 8-IN-1, 12-IN-1, ETC.): These models offer more than just air frying capabilities, such as roasting, baking, dehydrating, rotisserie, and even crisping and reheating. We should point out that while these functions can be helpful for some recipes, every single one of our recipes uses only the air fryer function.

The Toast Test: Calibrating Your Air Fryer

The amount of time a dish takes to cook can vary depending on the model, size, and wattage of an air fryer. That's why we recommend performing the Toast Test before making any recipes from this book, even if you're using the same air fryer we are (a 5.8-quart Cosori). We don't anticipate that your ideal cook time will be dramatically different from ours, but this easy exercise will at least clue you in as to whether your air fryer cooks more quickly or slowly than ours. That way you can anticipate whether you will need more or less cooking time for each recipe.

To perform the Toast Test, you'll need a single piece of white bread. Our air fryer will yield perfectly golden toast in 4 minutes at 400°F, which will be your baseline.

Place the bread in your basket and air fry at 400°F for 3 minutes. Check your toast: If it is not golden brown yet, air fry for 1 additional minute. Check again and keep adding more time as needed. (If you notice that your bread is getting knocked around by your air fryer's fan, which isn't too common but can happen, use a toothpick to help secure the bread in the basket.)

- If it takes 5 minutes for your toast to reach golden brown, you will know that you may need to add at least 1 extra minute to every 5 minutes of cook time for most of the recipes in this book. For example, if we suggest a cook time of 20 minutes, your air fryer may need 24 minutes.

- If it takes less than 4 minutes, then you may need to reduce the recipes' cooking time slightly so that your air fryer doesn't overcook the dishes.

Above all, treat these recipe cook times as *guidelines*. In most cases, we've included a range of time that each dish will need to cook to its ideal doneness, as well as indications that it's reached that point, whether it's by sight (e.g., bubbly, golden cheese) or internal temperature. Use your best judgment and go with what looks and feels right to you!

No Need to Use a Multifunction Air Fryer!

To make sure that anyone with an air fryer could enjoy these recipes, we developed every single one of these dishes—including our cookies and cakes!—using the "air fry" setting. Even if your air fryer has a "bake" or other specific setting, we encourage you to stick with the air fry setting to get the best results.

Upgrading Your Air Fryer Basket and Other Special Equipment

While many recipes in this book don't require anything more than the basket in your air fryer and kitchen gadgets that you most likely already have, there are some additional items that will allow you to use your air fryer for a wider variety of dishes and make your cooking (and cleanup) easier. These include:

- 7- or 8-inch springform pans
- 8-inch cake pan
- 7-inch Bundt pan
- 8-inch round casserole or baking dish (glass or silicone)
- 12 silicone muffin cups
- 8-inch wooden or metal skewers
- Four 3-inch (7-ounce) ramekins
- Air fryer grippers (for removing hot pans)
- Air fryer parchment paper (more optimal than regular parchment paper, as it has small holes that allow for better airflow)
- Meat thermometer
- 1½-inch portion scoop

A Guide to Cooking Oils and Fats

When cooking in your air fryer, it's important that you use an oil that is compatible with high-heat cooking. But before we get into what this means as well as what your options are, let's answer the one question that's most likely on your mind: *Wait a second, why do I need oil or fat? I thought the whole point of an air fryer is that I don't!* For most foods, applying a fat like oil or ghee (clarified butter) is what helps create a crisp, golden outside that locks in moisture and helps your item cook evenly. You definitely don't need to use oil in the same way or amount that you would to deep-fry foods, roast them in the oven, or sauté them on the stove, but you do still need a minimal amount when making most of these recipes. The only exception is when air frying frozen foods. That's because most of these items, such as tater tots, french fries, chicken nuggets, and pizza rolls, already have oil as a by-product of the manufacturing process.

Choosing an Oil or Fat

When choosing which oil or fat to use for a recipe, you need to consider its **smoke point**. This is the temperature at which the cooking heat causes the oil or fat to break down and smoke. To heat an oil or fat beyond its smoke point can make food taste not so great and cause—you guessed it— your kitchen to fill with smoke, neither of which you want when you're trying to cook dinner. Here is a list of our favorite cooking oils and fats, listed from our most recommended to least. Always be sure to check the cooking temperature called for in a recipe and use that to decide which oil or fat to use.

- AVOCADO OIL: 570°F smoke point
- GHEE (CLARIFIED BUTTER): 485°F smoke point
- EXTRA-LIGHT OLIVE OIL: 468°F smoke point
- SOYBEAN OIL: 460°F smoke point
- COCONUT OIL: 450°F smoke point
- PEANUT OIL: 450°F smoke point
- GRAPESEED OIL: 420°F smoke point
- VEGETABLE OIL: 400°F smoke point
- EXTRA-VIRGIN OLIVE OIL: 375°F smoke point
- BUTTER: 200° to 250°F smoke point

Nonstick Oil Spray

We do not recommend using a nonstick spray such as Pam when air frying. It will create a sticky, gummy surface in your basket and could compromise its nonstick properties. That said, some of our favorite cooking oils now come in a spray bottle, which is a nice way to apply a light coating of oil to your food.

How Much Oil Should I Use?

Every recipe is different, but the rule of thumb is to apply enough for a light coating both before cooking as well as after flipping (if applicable). For best results, use a small spray bottle and lightly spray the items. As we mentioned earlier, most processed foods that are being reheated from frozen will not need to be sprayed.

Common Cook Times and Temps

All of our recipes will include detailed cooking instructions and indications for doneness (including internal meat temperatures), but here is an at-a-glance resource for how long items typically take to cook in the air fryer (with the understanding that your model may differ slightly, see page 3). Cooking times are in Fahrenheit and may vary based on quantity, thickness of food, and type of air fryer.

FAQs

WHAT ARE THE ADVANTAGES OF AIR FRYING?
The air fryer offers a faster way to prepare foods (than an oven, stove top, or microwave) without needing to use an excess amount of oil. Foods can be cooked straight from frozen and will emerge perfectly cooked and/or crisp (depending on what you're cooking and your desired results).

WHY DO I HAVE CROSSOVER FOOD SMELLS?

Proper cleaning of your air fryer will ensure that leftover smells from previously cooked foods won't affect your current meal. Check your manufacturer guide to see if removable parts, such as the basket, tray, and racks, are dishwasher safe. Otherwise, clean with warm, soapy water. Also, don't forget to clean the inside of your air fryer after each use, which is just as important as cleaning the removable parts.

WHY DO I GET A "PLASTIC" SMELL IN THE AIR FRYER?

When using an air fryer for the first time, and possibly even during the first few weeks, you may notice a slight plastic or burning smell as the protective coating is exposed to heat. Just to be sure, check that all manufacturer packaging has been removed. If the problem continues, combine a tablespoon of vinegar with a tablespoon of lemon juice in a small ramekin. Air fry at 400°F for 3 to 5 minutes, then leave the ramekin in the basket until it cools. This should eliminate any plastic odors.

WHY IS THERE SMOKE COMING FROM THE AIR FRYER?

First, make sure you're using the right cooking oil or fat for your cooking temperature (see our handy list on page 6). Second, be sure to drain any excess fat from the bottom of the basket, which will smoke if not removed. We've included instructions in recipes where this is recommended.

More Tips and Tricks for Beginners

We asked our one-million-member-strong Facebook group for their biggest recommendations when it came to air frying, and we couldn't have said it better!

- If you are planning on using air fryer parchment paper, DO NOT place the parchment paper in the air fryer while preheating. Only place parchment paper into the air fryer *after* you have preheated the air fryer. Otherwise, the fan will blow the paper into the heating element and will burn.

- Make sure any lightweight ingredients are properly secured, including things like slices of bread and pepperoni slices. They can and often will end up flying around like dollar bills in one of those "grab the cash as it flies around the air" machines. While this doesn't happen often, and we've written our recipes to avoid this issue, if you over-stack your ingredients and they get too close to the fan, they might fly! You can use toothpicks to help secure items in the basket, or lay a small upside-down cooling rack directly on top of your items.

- To convert regular oven directions to your air fryer, the rule of thumb is to drop the temperature by 25°F and the time by about 20 percent. It may not always be this precise for your air fryer, so periodically check in on the item you're cooking.

- If you're feeling nervous about using your air fryer for the first time, start with something simple. Our Chicken Wings (page 97), Hard-Boiled Eggs (page 29), Ham and Cheese Frittata (page 18), and Steak and Veggie Fajitas (page 94) are all great places to start!

DON'T FORGET TO HAVE FUN!

The most important and helpful tip that we can give you is: Remember what this is all about—*making delicious meals*. A big reason why we love our air fryers so much is not only because all that time that they save in the kitchen makes food prep that much easier and more enjoyable but also because we can use that precious time to spend with our families (or ourselves) savoring every delicious bite. So go forth, pick a recipe, and get air frying!

Breakfast

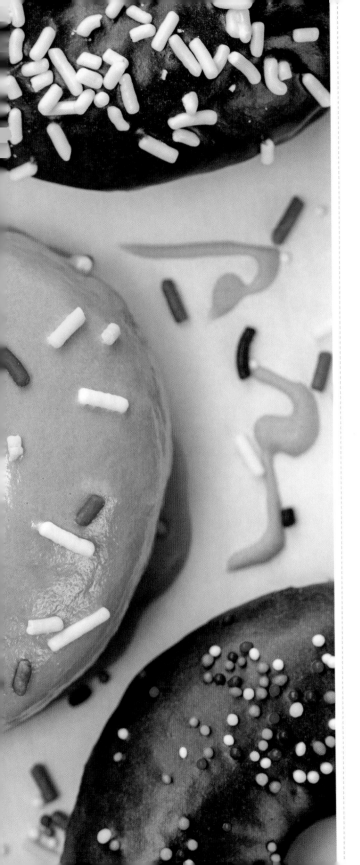

2

Most cookbooks divide their breakfast recipes into two categories: those that are lightning quick for weekdays, and those that require the luxury of a weekend's extra time. While we agree that quick and simple is typically best for the weekday morning scramble and that weekends are made for lazy mornings in the kitchen, we don't think that you should have to choose a breakfast dish based on how long it will take you to make it. Most of the recipes in this chapter require very little hands-on preparation and have relatively quick cook times. So while we love a Sunday brunch spread with Chocolate Chip Muffins (page 17) and Cinnamon Roll Casserole (page 22), we don't feel like we need to wait until the weekend to make something special. And as for those lightning-quick options that come in so handy? We've got you covered there, too.

Spinach and Feta Egg Bites

This is one workhorse of a recipe. Not only is it a delicious breakfast when made fresh, it is also a great make-ahead for those mornings where a home-cooked meal just isn't going to happen or when you need a snack on the go. Plus, you can customize these bites any way you like by adding different mix-ins or substituting any number of cheeses. It's the kind of staple that you can reach for every week, and it will never get old.

Makes 8 to 10 egg bites

6 large eggs	½ teaspoon kosher or sea salt
1 tablespoon whole milk	¼ teaspoon ground black pepper
½ cup chopped fresh spinach	6 cherry or grape tomatoes, chopped
¼ cup crumbled feta	Optional add-ins (see Note)

IN a large bowl, whisk together the eggs and milk. Add the spinach and cheese, along with the salt, pepper, tomatoes, and any additional add-ins (if using). Mix until the ingredients are evenly distributed in the egg mixture.

DIVIDE the mixture between 8 silicone muffin cups. They should be about two-thirds full, leaving room for them to rise while cooking.

ARRANGE the muffin cups in the air fryer basket. Air fry at 350°F for 2 minutes. Open the basket and gently stir the egg mixture with a fork to redistribute the ingredients, in case the fan has pushed them to the bottom. Continue cooking for another 6 to 8 minutes, until the eggs are cooked through and fluffy.

NOTE: *Feel free to get creative with the ingredients you add to these bites. Other great options include mushrooms, onions, bacon, bell peppers, ham, and jalapeños. You can also play with the types of cheese you use, such as swapping in Cheddar, mozzarella, or Swiss.*

Strawberry Scones

Many people will say that they don't love scones because they've only had the dry, crumbly ones that have been sitting around all day in a pastry case. But when they're prepared with a simple homemade dough, studded with fresh berries, and enjoyed freshly baked? That's a whole other story. We love serving these for brunch on the weekends and will play around with different berries in the mixture. Feel free to use what looks good at the market or whatever you have in the fridge.

Makes 8 scones

FOR THE SCONES

Avocado or olive oil cooking spray

2½ cups all-purpose flour, plus more for dusting

½ cup granulated sugar

2 teaspoons baking powder

1 teaspoon baking soda

½ teaspoon kosher or sea salt

½ cup (8 tablespoons) unsalted butter, sliced into tablespoons

¼ cup plus 1 tablespoon whole milk

¼ cup plain cream cheese

1 cup strawberries, chopped small

1 large egg

FOR THE GLAZE

1 cup powdered sugar

2 to 3 teaspoons whole milk

MAKE the scones: Lightly coat the air fryer basket with the cooking spray (see Note) and set aside.

IN a large bowl, combine the flour, sugar, baking powder, baking soda, and salt. Using a fork, press in the slices of butter until they're incorporated with the dry ingredients and the mixture forms a crumbly texture.

USING a hand mixer (or in the bowl of a stand mixer fitted with the paddle attachment), beat the ¼ cup of milk and the cream cheese on low to medium speed. Add the dry ingredients and mix until the ingredients are well combined and a soft dough forms. Use a wooden spoon or rubber spatula to gently fold in the strawberries until they are evenly combined.

LIGHTLY flour a clean work surface. Turn out the dough onto the surface and use a rolling pin to roll it into a ½-inch-thick circle.

(recipe continues)

CUT the dough into 8 even pie-shaped slices and arrange them in a single layer in the air fryer basket. You may need to work in batches.

IN a small bowl, whisk together the egg with the remaining 1 tablespoon milk. Brush the egg wash over the top of each scone. Air fry at 350°F for 6 to 8 minutes, until the scones are golden brown. Allow the scones to cool before topping with the glaze.

MAKE the glaze (see Note): In a small bowl, whisk together the powdered sugar and milk until no lumps remain. Once the scones have cooled, drizzle the glaze over the top.

THESE scones are best enjoyed fresh, but cooled scones can be stored in an airtight container in the refrigerator for 3 to 5 days.

NOTE: *For this recipe, we call for spraying the air fryer basket with cooking spray versus lining it with air fryer parchment paper. We've found that the parchment can keep the bottoms of the scones from cooking evenly with the tops. For an even quicker frosting option, melt ¼ cup storebought frosting for 15 to 30 seconds in the microwave until it is a good drizzling consistency. Drizzle over the scones.*

Chocolate Chip Muffins

Does it get better than a muffin that qualifies as breakfast but is chocolaty enough to pass for dessert? We don't think so either. These make a great addition to a brunch spread, are a quick and easy breakfast, or can be a lovely gesture like bringing them for a housewarming or a shower.

Makes 16 to 18 muffins

1¾ cups all-purpose flour

½ cup granulated sugar

1 teaspoon baking powder

¾ cup whole milk

¼ cup (4 tablespoons) unsalted butter, melted

1 large egg

1 cup mini chocolate chips (any type of chocolate)

FILL 18 silicone muffin cups with liners and set aside.

IN a medium bowl, whisk together the flour, sugar, and baking powder. Pour in the milk, butter, and egg, slowly stirring until an even batter forms. (Overmixing will result in a tougher muffin.) Use a wooden spoon or rubber spatula to fold in the chocolate chips until evenly distributed.

DIVIDE the batter between the prepared muffin cups until they're no more than three-quarters full (you may only get 16 or 17 muffins, and that's okay). Working in batches, if necessary, arrange the cups in the air fryer basket and air fry at 320°F for 10 to 12 minutes, until a toothpick or knife inserted in the center of a muffin comes out clean (aside from any smudges of chocolate).

ALLOW the muffins to cool slightly before removing them from the cups and placing them on a cooling rack to cool completely. The cooled muffins can be stored in an airtight container at room temperature for up to 3 days or frozen for up to 3 months.

Ham and Cheese Frittata

Frittatas are the ideal breakfast recipe because they're extremely easy to make (even first thing in the morning) and are a great canvas for all kinds of ingredients. For this version, we're going with a classic flavor combination of ham and cheese plus bell peppers and green onions. However, feel free to change up the mix-ins to suit your tastes or whatever needs using up in the fridge.

Serves 6 to 8

Avocado or olive oil cooking spray

6 large eggs

¼ cup whole milk

½ cup diced cooked ham

½ cup shredded mild or medium Cheddar

¼ cup shredded Gruyère (Swiss will work, too)

¼ cup diced green bell pepper

2 tablespoons finely chopped green onion (green part only)

½ teaspoon kosher or sea salt

¼ teaspoon ground black pepper

LIGHTLY coat an 8-inch round casserole or baking dish (glass or silicone) with cooking spray and set aside.

IN a medium bowl, whisk together the eggs and milk until well combined. Stir in the ham, cheeses, bell pepper, onion, salt, and black pepper.

POUR the egg mixture into the prepared dish and place it in the air fryer basket. Air fry at 350°F for 5 minutes. Give the ingredients a stir (to help keep them evenly mixed as the air fryer fan blows on them), then continue cooking for another 10 to 12 minutes, until the eggs are firmly cooked. Serve warm.

Doughnuts

There is no joy like a hot, fresh-from-the-fryer doughnut. So imagine how excited we are to tell you that you can re-create that very same feeling at home—and with zero deep-frying. Thanks to this recipe, you'll get the fluffy, yeasted center and crispy, golden outside you'd expect from the very best doughnut shop.

Makes 1 dozen doughnuts

---

1 cup whole milk

¼ cup granulated sugar

1 (¼-ounce) packet or 2¼ teaspoons instant yeast

¼ teaspoon kosher or sea salt

3 cups all-purpose flour, plus more for dusting

2 tablespoons unsalted butter, melted

1 large egg, beaten

1 teaspoon vanilla extract

Avocado or olive oil cooking spray

IN a microwave-safe bowl or small pot over low heat, heat the milk until warm (about 120°F).

IN a medium bowl, combine the warmed milk, sugar, yeast, and salt. Let the mixture sit for 3 to 5 minutes, until the yeast begins to bubble. Add the flour, butter, egg, and vanilla and stir until a soft dough forms.

TURN out the dough onto a clean work surface that's been lightly dusted with flour. Knead the dough until it thickens slightly and is smooth to the touch, about 5 minutes. Shape the dough into a ball and place it in a large bowl that's been lightly coated with cooking spray. Cover the bowl with plastic wrap and let the dough rest in a warm place until it doubles in size, 45 minutes to an hour.

PUNCH down the dough to release the air and once again turn it out onto a lightly floured work surface. Use a rolling pin to roll out the dough to about ½-inch thickness. Use a 3-inch doughnut cutter to cut out 12 doughnuts. (You could also do this with a 3-inch cookie cutter and a bottle cap or paring knife to remove the middle.)

ARRANGE the doughnuts in a single layer in the air fryer basket. (You may need to work in batches.) Lightly spray them with the cooking oil and air fry at 320°F for 6 to 8 minutes, until the tops are golden brown. Flip over the doughnuts and cook for an additional 2 to 3 minutes, until the second side is golden brown. Serve hot.

Cinnamon Roll Casserole

This recipe takes store-bought cinnamon rolls and gives them a decadent homemade spin. We love serving this rich, gooey dish for special breakfast occasions like birthdays, family get-togethers, and the holidays, and it's always a hit. You can serve this drizzled with the icing packet that comes with most cans of cinnamon rolls, make our simple recipe below, or use maple syrup for more of a french toast flavor.

Serves 4

FOR THE CINNAMON ROLLS

1 (12.4-ounce) can cinnamon rolls

2 large eggs

¼ cup whole milk (see Note)

1 teaspoon ground cinnamon

1 teaspoon vanilla extract

FOR THE ICING (OPTIONAL)

1 cup powdered sugar

3 tablespoons whole milk

1 teaspoon vanilla extract

Maple syrup, for serving (optional)

MAKE the cinnamon rolls: Line the air fryer basket with an 8-inch round casserole or baking dish (glass or silicone). Set aside.

CUT each of the cinnamon rolls into 6 pieces and arrange them in a single layer in the prepared air fryer basket. Set aside.

IN a medium bowl, whisk together the eggs, milk, cinnamon, and vanilla. Pour the mixture over the cinnamon rolls.

AIR fry at 310°F for 16 to 18 minutes, stirring every 3 to 5 minutes, until the eggs are set. Stirring periodically helps ensure that the mixture continues to set while not overcooking the cinnamon rolls.

MAKE the icing (if using): In a medium bowl, whisk together the powdered sugar with 2 tablespoons of the milk and the vanilla. If the icing is still too thick to drizzle well, add the remaining 1 tablespoon milk.

IF desired, drizzle the icing or the maple syrup over the top of the cinnamon rolls and serve warm.

NOTE: *For a richer, creamier version of this recipe, use ¼ cup of heavy cream in place of the milk.*

Easy Breakfast (or Anytime) Biscuits

Everybody gets excited about a basket of just-baked biscuits on the table. While you could just go to the store and buy a canister to pop into the oven, it will never come close to homemade—and not many of us have time for that on a regular basis. Luckily, this recipe requires very little hands-on time and yields the lightest, fluffiest biscuits. Serve these as part of a breakfast or brunch spread, or alongside a main dish for dinner.

Makes 8 to 10 biscuits

---

2 cups all-purpose flour, plus more for dusting

1 tablespoon baking powder

2 teaspoons granulated sugar

½ teaspoon kosher or sea salt

½ cup (8 tablespoons) unsalted butter, sliced

½ cup sour cream

¼ cup plus 1 tablespoon whole milk

Avocado or olive oil cooking spray

1 large egg

IN a medium bowl, combine the flour, baking powder, sugar, and salt. Use a fork to mix well. Add the butter and continue mixing and pressing the butter into the flour until the mixture is flaky. Slowly stir in the sour cream and ¼ cup of the milk until the dough becomes thick and smooth.

LIGHTLY flour a clean work surface and turn out the dough. Lightly knead the dough until smooth, 2 to 3 minutes. Use a rolling pin to roll out the dough to about 1-inch thickness.

USE a 3½-inch biscuit cutter or the rim of a glass to cut out as many biscuits as you can. Gather up the scraps, roll out again, and cut out additional biscuits (you'll have 8 to 10). Arrange the biscuits in a single layer in the air fryer basket and lightly coat them with the cooking spray. You may need to do this in batches.

IN a small bowl, whisk together the egg and the remaining 1 tablespoon milk. Brush the tops of the biscuits with the egg wash. Air fry at 350°F for 8 to 10 minutes, until the biscuits have puffed up and are slightly golden on top.

French Toast Casserole

We love having a stash of recipes in our back pocket for those mornings when we can take a little bit more time to prepare a decadent breakfast. We've been known to surprise the kids on the weekends with this dish or put it out as part of a holiday or brunch spread. It's perfect alongside fresh fruit and a side of bacon.

Serves 4 to 6

2 large eggs

¼ cup whole milk

2 teaspoons granulated sugar

1½ teaspoons ground cinnamon

½ loaf of white bread (8 to 10 slices; see Note), cut into 1-inch cubes (2 to 3 cups) and left at room temperature for 1 hour

Maple syrup, for serving

Powdered sugar, for serving

IN a medium bowl, whisk the eggs. Add the milk, sugar, and cinnamon and whisk to combine. Add the bread cubes and use a spatula to gently press on the bread to ensure that it has all been coated by the egg mixture.

TRANSFER the mixture to an 8-inch round casserole or baking dish (glass or silicone). Air fry at 330°F for 9 minutes, until golden brown and slightly crispy on top. Carefully remove the baking dish from the air fryer basket and top the french toast with maple syrup and powdered sugar.

NOTE: *French bread or brioche would also work nicely in this recipe.*

Breakfast Pizza

There are about a million ways you can make eggs in the morning, but have you tried 'em on a pizza? We love this dish because it's easy enough for a quick morning meal but impressive enough for a decadent lazy morning or brunch. Feel free to customize your pizza with your favorite toppings!

Serves 2

Avocado or olive oil cooking spray, or extra-virgin olive oil

All-purpose flour, for dusting

1 (13.8-ounce) can refrigerated pizza dough

3 large eggs, beaten

½ cup cooked and crumbled Italian sausage

½ cup diced ham

4 cherry tomatoes, halved

1 tablespoon chopped green onion (green part only)

½ cup shredded or torn mozzarella

½ cup shredded mild or medium Cheddar

LIGHTLY coat an 8-inch round casserole or baking dish (glass or silicone) with cooking spray or oil.

DUST a clean work surface with flour and roll out the dough to roughly match the size of your air fryer basket. Roll the edges inward by about 1 inch to create a crust.

CAREFULLY transfer the dough to the prepared dish and set it in the air fryer basket. Air fry at 350°F for 5 minutes, or until the top of the dough is lightly browned.

REMOVE the air fryer basket and evenly top the dough with the eggs, followed by the sausage, ham, tomatoes, green onion, and cheeses.

COOK at 350°F for 5 to 8 minutes, until the cheese is golden brown and the dough has crisp edges. Serve hot.

Hard-Boiled Eggs

Now you can finally nail the perfect hard-boiled egg. We love making a batch of these and keeping them in the fridge as the ultimate staple. They last for up to a week and can be grabbed for breakfast or a snack, chopped into a salad, whipped with mayo, sprinkled over veggies, or transformed into a platter of deviled eggs.

Makes 6 eggs

Ice	6 large eggs (see Note)

IN a medium bowl, combine a handful of ice with cold water and set aside.

PLACE the eggs in the air fryer basket and cook at 270°F for 17 minutes. Carefully transfer the eggs to the ice bath to cool for 10 minutes. Remove the eggs and gently peel the outer shell. (You could also leave the shell on, if you prefer.)

THE eggs can be stored in an airtight container in the refrigerator for up to 7 days.

NOTE: *If possible, use older eggs for this preparation. Fresh, new eggs can be more difficult to peel. And don't be tempted to skip the ice bath! It brings the temperature of the eggs down, which keeps them from overcooking. It also makes peeling them easier.*

Cheese and Mushroom Omelet

Our favorite part about making an omelet in the air fryer is how easy it is to set it and forget it—a major improvement from needing to babysit it on the stove! And yet you still get the same fluffy and flavorful results. Feel free to play around with the mix-ins to customize this omelet to your family's preferences or to change up your morning menu.

Serves 2

Avocado or olive oil cooking spray

3 large eggs

1 tablespoon whole milk

2 tablespoons diced white onion

2 tablespoons diced red bell pepper

2 portobello or white mushrooms, sliced

Kosher or sea salt and ground black pepper

1 tablespoon chopped green onion (green part only)

3 tablespoons shredded mild or medium Cheddar

LIGHTLY coat an 8-inch round casserole or baking dish (glass or silicone) with cooking spray and set aside.

IN a medium bowl, whisk together the eggs and milk. Stir in the white onion and bell pepper.

POUR the egg mixture into the prepared dish and top with the sliced mushrooms. Place the dish into the air fryer basket and air fry at 350°F for 5 minutes.

SPRINKLE the top of the eggs with a pinch of salt and pepper, followed by the green onion. Top with the Cheddar and air fry for another 3 to 4 minutes, until the cheese has melted. Carefully remove the omelet from the pan with a spatula and serve.

Chicken and Waffle Scramble

You can't talk about breakfast without talking about chicken and waffles. It's a standby Southern comfort food dish that we've made even more satisfying with the addition of scrambled eggs (yes, you can make that in the air fryer, too!). This recipe would be perfect for a weekend brunch but is quick enough to come together for a fast weekday breakfast. Not to mention breakfast for dinner!

Serves 4

4 frozen blackened chicken breast strips

3 frozen waffles

3 large eggs

2 tablespoons whole milk

Maple syrup, for serving

ARRANGE the chicken and waffles in a single layer in the air fryer basket (you may need to work in batches). Air fry at 400°F for 6 minutes, until the waffles are golden and the middle of the chicken registers 165°F on an instant-read thermometer.

WHILE the chicken and waffles cook, whisk together the eggs and milk in a small bowl. Set aside.

REMOVE the chicken and waffles from the air fryer basket and place an 8-inch round casserole or baking dish (glass or silicone) into the basket. Pour the egg mixture into the dish and air fry at 350°F for 4 minutes, stirring occasionally. You want the eggs to be scrambled but still undercooked.

TEAR the waffles and cut the chicken into bite-sized pieces. Add the chicken and waffles to the pan with the scrambled eggs and cook for an additional 2 to 3 minutes, until the eggs are fully cooked.

CAREFULLY remove the pan from the air fryer and serve the scramble with maple syrup.

Chicken and Hash Brown Breakfast Casserole

Imagine all your favorite breakfast trimmings—sausage, hash browns, egg, cheese—baked up in one delicious dish. Well, we're happy to be the first to tell you that dreams do come true. And in under 20 minutes!

Serves 4

Avocado or olive oil cooking spray

6 ounces chicken sausage, chopped

6 ounces frozen diced hash brown potatoes

¼ cup diced white onion

4 large eggs

¼ cup whole milk

¾ cup shredded mild or medium Cheddar

Kosher or sea salt and ground black pepper

PREHEAT the air fryer to 400°F. Lightly coat the inside of an 8-inch round casserole or baking dish (glass or silicone) with cooking spray and set aside. Lightly coat the air fryer basket with cooking spray or line it with a silicone baking mat.

ADD the sausage, potatoes, and onion to the air fryer basket and toss to combine. Air fry at 400°F for 6 minutes, tossing occasionally. The sausages and potatoes should be browned and cooked through.

WHILE the sausage, potatoes, and onion cook, whisk together the eggs and milk in a medium bowl. Pour the mixture into the prepared baking dish. Top with the sausage mixture and ½ cup of the cheese.

PLACE the baking dish in the air fryer basket, no need to wipe out the basket first, and air fry at 350°F for 7 minutes, using a fork to scramble the mixture halfway through. Top the casserole with the remaining ¼ cup cheese, sprinkle with salt and pepper, and air fry for another 3 minutes. The eggs should be set and the cheese melted. Serve hot.

NOTE: *Consider changing up the flavors by adding in ¼ cup diced green chiles and an additional ½ teaspoon of ground black pepper for extra spice.*

Tater Tot Casserole

We've always loved tater tots because they're essentially mini hash browns (and who doesn't love crispy fried potatoes?). So we decided to take them, along with fellow breakfast staples eggs and bacon, and create a fun morning casserole. And the biggest bonus is that it comes together more quickly than if you made each component separately.

Serves 4

---

8 slices of bacon	¼ cup whole milk
20 frozen tater tots	½ teaspoon kosher or sea salt
4 large eggs	¼ teaspoon ground black pepper
½ cup shredded mild or medium Cheddar	2 tablespoons chopped green onion (green part only)

LAY the bacon in a single layer in the air fryer basket and air fry at 400°F for 8 to 10 minutes, until crisp. Transfer the bacon to a paper towel–lined plate and set aside.

PLACE the tater tots in the air fryer basket—no need to wipe it out first—and air fry at 400°F for 10 minutes, until golden and crispy. Transfer the tater tots to a plate and set them aside to cool.

IN a medium bowl, whisk together the eggs, cheese, milk, salt, and pepper. Pour the egg mixture into an 8-inch round casserole or baking dish (glass or silicone) and set the dish inside the air fryer basket. Air fry at 350°F for 9 to 11 minutes, stirring about halfway, until the eggs are cooked through and the cheese has melted.

WHILE the eggs cook, roughly chop the cooled tater tots and crumble the bacon. When the eggs are done, top them with the chopped tater tots and crumbled bacon. Return the basket to the air fryer and cook for another 3 minutes. Sprinkle with the green onion and serve.

Pizza and Pasta

3

While we don't exactly get any joy out of proving people wrong . . . let's just say we get a little thrill anytime someone says you can't make the perfect pizza or pasta dish in the air fryer. These recipes are *exactly* the kind of fare that these machines were made for, whether you're heaping dough with all of your favorite toppings or layering up all manner of pasta with sauces and other mix-ins. The truth is, there's just nothing an air fryer can't do, and your comfort food go-tos are all the better for it.

Ravioli Bake

This recipe is a favorite of ours because it combines easy-to-find store-bought ingredients but elevates them into a saucy, cheesy meal that could easily be from your favorite Italian restaurant. It doesn't ask too much of you to put it all together—always appreciated when running in the door just before dinnertime—and feels familiar and comforting at the end of a long day.

Serves 4

---

1 cup prepared or store-bought tomato basil sauce

1½ cups shredded mozzarella

1 (9-ounce) package store-bought cheese ravioli (about 20 ravioli)

20 slices of pepperoni

Kosher or sea salt and freshly ground black pepper

Chopped fresh parsley, for garnish

IN an 8-inch round casserole or baking dish (glass or silicone), spread 3 tablespoons of the tomato sauce over the bottom of the dish.

USE one-third of the cheese to create a layer over the sauce, followed by half of the ravioli. Top each ravioli with a slice of pepperoni. Sprinkle over another one-third of the cheese, followed by the remaining ravioli and pepperoni. Add a layer of the remaining tomato sauce, followed by a final layer of the remaining cheese. Season with salt and pepper.

PLACE the dish into the air fryer basket and air fry at 350°F for 8 to 10 minutes, until the cheese is melted and golden. Carefully remove the dish from the air fryer and top with chopped parsley before serving.

Baked Spaghetti

Somewhere between a lasagna and a casserole, you'll find this baked spaghetti. It has buttery layers of noodles topped with meat sauce and, of course, lots of cheese. It's the perfect crowd-pleasing dinner and the kind of leftovers you start looking forward to at breakfast.

Serves 4 to 6

Avocado or olive oil cooking spray, or extra-virgin olive oil

½ pound lean ground beef

1 cup tomato sauce

1 tablespoon dried oregano

½ teaspoon ground black pepper

1 cup ricotta

½ cup plain cream cheese

¼ cup sour cream

8 ounces spaghetti, cooked according to the package instructions and drained

½ cup (8 tablespoons) salted butter, sliced into tablespoons

½ cup shredded mild Cheddar

½ cup shredded or torn mozzarella

2 teaspoons chopped fresh parsley leaves, for garnish

LIGHTLY coat an 8-inch round casserole or baking dish (glass or silicone) with the cooking spray or oil and set aside.

IN a large skillet over medium heat, cook the beef, while breaking it up with a spoon or spatula, until it is no longer pink, about 5 minutes. Drain the fat from the pan. Stir in the tomato sauce, oregano, and pepper and set aside.

IN a small bowl, stir together the ricotta, cream cheese, and sour cream.

ADD half of the cooked spaghetti to the prepared baking dish. Evenly top the spaghetti with half of the butter, then spread the ricotta mixture over the spaghetti and butter. Add the remaining spaghetti, then the remaining butter. Pour the meat sauce over the spaghetti and top with the Cheddar and mozzarella.

COVER the pan with foil and air fry at 350°F for 30 minutes. Remove the foil and air fry at 280°F for another 15 minutes, until the cheese is melted and golden brown. Allow the spaghetti to cool for 10 minutes before serving. Garnish with the fresh parsley, slice, and serve.

Mediterranean Pizza with Olives, Feta, and Onion

This recipe takes one of our favorite Mediterranean dishes, the Greek salad, and combines it with another staple in our kitchen: pizza. It might seem like a surprising combination, but you'll love the way the traditional mozzarella is complemented by tangy feta and olives, fresh tomatoes, and red onion that gets sweetly caramelized as they cook. Plus, who doesn't love a pizza that comes with its own built-in salad?!

Serves 2

Avocado or olive oil cooking spray (optional)

1 teaspoon extra-virgin olive oil, plus more for the basket if not using cooking spray or parchment paper

All-purpose flour, for dusting

1 (13.8-ounce) can refrigerated pizza dough

½ teaspoon minced garlic

2 tablespoons pizza sauce

½ cup shredded or torn mozzarella

8 cherry or grape tomatoes, halved

¼ cup crumbled feta

4 pitted kalamata or black olives, chopped or halved

1 to 2 tablespoons finely chopped red onion (depending on how much you like onion!)

4 fresh basil leaves, torn

LIGHTLY coat the air fryer basket with cooking spray, oil, or parchment paper. Preheat the air fryer to 370°F.

DUST a clean work surface with flour and roll out the dough to roughly match the size of your air fryer basket. Roll the edges inward by about 1 inch to create a crust. Carefully transfer the dough to the air fryer basket and set aside.

IN a small bowl, combine the olive oil and garlic. Lightly brush the top of the crust with the mixture. Spread the pizza sauce over the garlic and oil so it's evenly covering the bottom of the pizza crust.

EVENLY top the pizza with the mozzarella, tomatoes, feta, olives, and onion. Air fry for 9 to 11 minutes, until the crust is golden brown and the cheese has melted. Scatter the basil over the top and serve.

Balsamic and Goat Cheese Pizza

We couldn't decide what's to love more about this dish—the fact that you can make delicious pizza in your air fryer using store-bought pizza dough (doesn't get much easier than that!), OR that it gives any restaurant-made version a run for its money. With its combination of sweet, caramelized onion, creamy goat cheese, and spicy arugula, this pizza would be just as great for an easy dinner for family as it would be for entertaining guests. You could also slice it up and serve it as part of an appetizer spread.

Serves 2

Avocado or olive oil cooking spray (optional)

1 tablespoon extra-virgin olive oil, plus more for the basket if not using cooking spray or parchment paper

½ medium red onion, quartered and sliced thin (about ½ cup)

1 tablespoon balsamic vinegar

1 tablespoon packed brown sugar

All-purpose flour, for dusting

1 (13.8-ounce) can refrigerated pizza dough

¼ cup crumbled goat cheese

½ cup packed arugula, stems removed, and torn or chopped

LIGHTLY coat the air fryer basket with cooking spray, olive oil, or parchment paper. Preheat the air fryer to 370°F.

IN a medium sauté pan over medium heat, add the olive oil and onions. Cook, stirring frequently, until the onion starts to turn light brown, 1 to 2 minutes. Add the balsamic vinegar and brown sugar and continue cooking and stirring until the onion is golden and caramelized, 3 to 5 minutes. Remove the pan from the heat and set aside.

PREHEAT the air fryer to 370°F.

DUST a clean work surface with flour and roll out the dough until it is roughly the size of your air fryer basket. Roll the edges inward by about 1 inch to create a crust. Carefully transfer the dough to the prepared basket.

EVENLY spread the caramelized onion over the dough. Top with the goat cheese and arugula.

AIR fry for 9 to 11 minutes, until the crust is golden brown. Use a spatula to gently transfer the pizza to a cutting board. Slice and enjoy hot.

Pesto, Ham, and Swiss Pizza

Pizza night is always a big hit at our houses, especially when we get creative with the toppings. We took the always-classic pairing of smoky ham and Swiss and teamed it up with garlicky, basil-y pesto. It's made a convert of even the most die-hard margherita fans!

Serves 2

Avocado or olive oil cooking spray or extra-virgin olive oil, for greasing

All-purpose flour, for dusting

1 (13.8-ounce) can refrigerated pizza dough

2 tablespoons prepared or store-bought basil pesto

⅓ cup diced smoked ham

¼ cup shredded Swiss

¼ cup shredded or torn mozzarella

¼ cup chopped baby spinach

3 fresh basil leaves, torn

LIGHTLY coat the air fryer basket with cooking spray, oil, or parchment paper. Preheat the air fryer to 370°F.

DUST a clean work surface with flour and roll out the dough until it is roughly the size of your air fryer basket. Roll the edges inward by about 1 inch to create a crust. Carefully transfer the dough to the prepared basket.

BRUSH the pesto evenly over the dough, avoiding the edges that will be the crust. Top with the ham, Swiss, mozzarella, spinach, and basil.

AIR fry at 370°F for 9 to 11 minutes, until the crust is golden and crisp and the cheese has melted. Use a spatula to carefully transfer the pizza to a cutting board and slice. Enjoy hot.

Chicken Ranchero Pizza

Sure, there's a time for classic pepperoni, sausage, or plain cheese, but we think pizza night can sometimes use a little refresh. For this fun new option, we've swapped out pizza sauce for a creamy Alfredo sauce, which gets heaped with chicken, peppers, jalapeños, and, of course, lots of cheese. Don't be surprised when DIY pizza night gets requested a lot more often than ordering delivery.

Serves 2

Avocado or olive oil cooking spray (optional)

1 teaspoon extra-virgin olive oil, plus more for the basket if not using cooking spray or parchment paper

All-purpose flour, for dusting

1 (13.8-ounce) can refrigerated pizza dough

3 tablespoons store-bought Alfredo sauce

¼ cup cooked, cubed chicken

1 tablespoon diced green bell pepper

1 teaspoon sliced or diced jalapeño

½ teaspoon ground black pepper

¾ cup shredded or torn mozzarella

LIGHTLY coat the air fryer basket with cooking spray, oil, or parchment paper. Preheat the air fryer to 370°F.

DUST a clean work surface with flour and roll out the dough until it is roughly the size of your air fryer basket. Roll the edges inward by about 1 inch to create a crust. Carefully transfer the dough to the prepared basket.

BRUSH the top with the oil. Spread an even layer of the Alfredo sauce over the pizza, leaving a 1- to 2-inch crust around the border. Top the sauce with the chicken, bell pepper, jalapeño, and black pepper. Sprinkle everything with the cheese.

AIR fry at 370°F for 9 to 11 minutes, until the crust is golden and crisp and the cheese has melted. Use a spatula to carefully transfer the pizza to a cutting board and slice. Enjoy hot.

Supreme Calzones

If you've never been fortunate enough to have tried a calzone, imagine the ultimate pizza pocket stuffed full of your favorite toppings. Sounds pretty amazing, right? The great news is that they're incredibly easy to make at home; all you need is store-bought pizza dough, sauce, cheese, and anything you like to dress up your pie. Less than 10 minutes later, you'll have a pizzeria-worthy dish.

Makes 2 large calzones or 4 medium calzones

Avocado or olive oil cooking spray or extra-virgin olive oil, for greasing

1 (13.8-ounce) can refrigerated pizza dough

All-purpose flour, for dusting

2 tablespoons pizza sauce, plus more (optional) for serving

1 cup shredded or torn mozzarella

4 large or 6 standard-sized slices of pepperoni (optional)

2 to 3 tablespoons finely chopped green bell peppers (optional)

2 to 3 tablespoons sliced black olives (optional)

2 to 3 tablespoons finely chopped red onion (optional)

¼ cup grated Parmesan

Marinara sauce, for serving (optional)

LIGHTLY coat the air fryer basket with cooking spray, oil, or parchment paper. Preheat the air fryer to 370°F.

DIVIDE the dough in half if making 2 large calzones or into quarters if making 4 medium ones. Lightly flour a clean work surface and use a rolling pin to roll the dough to ¼-inch thickness.

EVENLY spread the pizza sauce over one half of each circle of dough, leaving a 1-inch border. Top the sauce with the mozzarella, followed by your desired toppings. Fold the plain half of the dough over the toppings and pinch the edges together to seal, or crimp them together with a fork.

CAREFULLY transfer the calzones to the basket in a single layer, working in batches if necessary. Air fry for 7 to 9 minutes, until the crust is golden and crisp.

TOP with the Parmesan and serve with pizza or marinara sauce, if desired.

Chicken Parm Bites

These cheesy, crispy bites of chicken are exactly what they sound like—bite-sized chicken Parms. They're so flavorful that you barely need anything else to round out the dish. You can toss them with pasta and marinara or plain buttered noodles for dinner, or you can serve them on their own as an appetizer.

Serves 4

2 tablespoons all-purpose flour

1 teaspoon garlic powder

1 teaspoon ground black pepper

1½ pounds boneless, skinless chicken breast, cut into 1-inch cubes

1 tablespoon extra-virgin olive oil

Avocado or olive oil cooking spray

3 tablespoons grated Parmesan

1 teaspoon dried parsley flakes

IN a small bowl, combine the flour, garlic powder, and black pepper. Mix well.

IN a medium bowl, toss chicken with the olive oil to coat. Add the flour mixture and toss until each cube of chicken is well coated.

ADD the chicken to the air fryer basket in a single layer and lightly coat with the cooking spray. Air fry at 360°F for 10 minutes. Flip each piece of chicken and air fry for another 6 to 8 minutes, until golden brown. Sprinkle the chicken with the Parmesan and air fry for 1 additional minute. Top with the parsley and serve as desired.

Classic Lasagna

At first, it might seem like there's not much to say about this classic-for-a-reason lasagna, but that just wouldn't be like us! We've given this dish an update by including both Italian sausage and ground beef in the sauce. And by reconfiguring the recipe for the air fryer, we've provided you with one more dependable "wow" dish for your weekly dinner lineup.

Serves 4

Avocado or olive oil cooking spray

½ pound ground Italian sausage

½ pound lean ground beef

1 (24-ounce) jar marinara sauce

1 cup ricotta

1 large egg

¼ cup Cheddar

1½ cups shredded or torn mozzarella

½ cup shredded or grated Parmesan

10 ounces oven-ready lasagna noodles

3 tablespoons chopped fresh flat-leaf parsley leaves

LIGHTLY coat an 8-inch round casserole or baking dish (glass or silicone) with cooking spray and set aside.

IN a large skillet over medium-high heat, combine the Italian sausage and ground beef. Cook while breaking them up with your spoon, until brown, about 5 minutes. Stir in the marinara and set aside.

IN a medium bowl, whisk together the ricotta cheese and the egg. In a small bowl, toss together the Cheddar, mozzarella, and Parmesan.

SPREAD a thin layer of the meat sauce over the bottom of the prepared baking dish. Top with a layer of the noodles, then spread half of the ricotta mixture over the noodles. Sprinkle ½ cup of the Cheddar, mozzarella, and Parmesan over the top.

REPEAT the pattern twice more with ½ cup meat sauce, followed by noodles, the remaining half of the ricotta mixture, and ½ cup cheese. For the final layer, use the remainder of the meat sauce topped with the remainder of the cheese.

COVER the pan with foil and place it in the air fryer basket. Air fry at 360°F for 35 minutes. Remove the foil and air fry for an additional 15 minutes, or until the top layer of cheese is golden brown.

REMOVE the baking dish from the air fryer and allow the lasagna to rest for 10 minutes. Top with the parsley before slicing and serving.

Burgers, Sliders, and Sandwiches

4

If you're eager to see just what your air fryer can do, look no further than this chapter. Whether it's taking the place of a grill, griddle, or panini press, the air fryer is nothing short of sandwich-making magic. From turkey patties stuffed with cheese, to crispy chicken sliders, to the ultimate grilled cheese, these recipes just made lunch and dinner a whole lot quicker and tastier.

Stuffed Turkey Burgers

It's one thing to have perfectly juicy burgers without even having to preheat a grill, but it's quite another for those patties to be bursting with melted provolone and sandwiched between your favorite toppings on a brioche bun. It's safe to say that your burger game just leveled up.

Serves 4

Avocado or olive oil cooking spray (optional)

1 pound ground turkey

½ cup Italian-seasoned bread crumbs

1 large egg

¼ cup chopped green onion (green part only)

4 slices of provolone

4 brioche buns

Sliced tomatoes, for serving (optional)

Lettuce, for serving (optional)

Pickles, for serving (optional)

Your favorite burger dressings and condiments, for serving

LIGHTLY coat the air fryer basket with cooking spray or line it with air fryer parchment paper and set aside.

IN a large bowl, combine the turkey, bread crumbs, and egg. Mix well. Fold in the green onion until evenly distributed in the mixture.

DIVIDE the meat mixture into 8 even portions and roll each into a ball. Fold one slice of cheese into quarters, then place the folded cheese on top of one of the meat balls. Cover the cheese with a second meat ball and pinch the sides together to completely cover and seal in the cheese. Shape the meat into a patty and set aside. Repeat with the remaining meat and cheese until you have 4 stuffed patties.

ARRANGE the patties in a single layer in the prepared basket. Air fry at 360°F for 13 to 15 minutes, flipping the patties halfway. The burgers are done when an instant-read thermometer inserted in the middle reads 165°F. Serve on a bun with your favorite burger toppings, dressings, and condiments.

Teriyaki Bison Burgers

We're big fans of using ground bison instead of beef for our burgers because it packs some serious protein and yet it's nice and lean. Because bison can be a little dry—and because pineapple makes everything better (it especially reminds us of tropical beaches, piña coladas, and Dole Whip at Disney), we decided to add it to the mix. Combined with sweet-savory teriyaki, pineapple just takes this dish over the top.

Serves 4

1 pound ground bison

¼ cup sliced green onion (green part only)

¼ cup chopped pineapple (optional)

2 tablespoons Homemade Teriyaki Sauce (recipe follows) or store-bought, plus more for serving

1 tablespoon pineapple juice

1 teaspoon minced garlic (about 2 medium cloves)

1 teaspoon grated fresh ginger

4 hamburger buns

4 pineapple rings

Your favorite burger toppings (optional)

IN a large bowl, combine the bison with the green onion, chopped pineapple (if using), teriyaki sauce, pineapple juice, garlic, and ginger. Use your hands or a spoon to mix until the ingredients are evenly incorporated.

SHAPE the meat mixture into 4 burger patties. Arrange the patties in the air fryer basket in a single layer and air fry at 380°F for 8 minutes. Flip the patties and continue cooking for an additional 4 minutes. An instant-read thermometer inserted in the middle of a patty should read 160°F.

TO build the burgers, place a patty on the bottom bun and top with a pineapple ring, a drizzle of teriyaki sauce, and any other of your favorite burger toppings. Serve immediately.

Homemade Teriyaki Sauce

Makes about 1 cup

1 tablespoon cornstarch

¼ cup pineapple juice

¼ cup packed brown sugar

2 tablespoons soy sauce

1 teaspoon minced garlic (about 2 medium cloves)

1 teaspoon grated fresh ginger

IN a small bowl, mix the cornstarch with ½ cup water until the cornstarch dissolves. Set aside.

IN a small saucepan over medium heat, combine the pineapple juice, brown sugar, soy sauce, garlic, and ginger. When the mixture begins to boil, whisk in the cornstarch mixture. Continue whisking for 2 to 3 minutes, until the sauce has thickened slightly. (It will continue to thicken as it cools.) Remove the pan from the heat.

ALLOW the sauce to cool completely, then store in the refrigerator in an airtight container for up to 3 days.

BBQ Beef Sandwiches

When you think of a great BBQ sandwich, you usually think of meat smoked for hours until it's impossibly tender, then braised with a deeply flavored sauce that someone's great-grandmother passed down the recipe for. Well, lucky for you, we're about to cut that time down to just a handful of minutes because thinly sliced steak or roast beef slathered in a four-ingredient sauce and tossed in the air fryer will yield the same mouthwatering results.

Serves 4

¼ cup ketchup

2 tablespoons packed brown sugar

2 teaspoons Dijon mustard

2 teaspoons Worcestershire sauce

1 pound roast beef or cooked steak, thinly sliced

4 brioche buns, french bread rolls, or hamburger buns

IN a small bowl, mix together the ketchup, brown sugar, mustard, and Worcestershire sauce.

IN a medium bowl, toss the meat with half of the sauce. Transfer the mixture to the air fryer basket and air fry at 400°F for 4 to 6 minutes, until the meat is heated through.

TRANSFER the cooked mixture back to the medium bowl and toss with the remaining sauce. Divide the BBQ beef between the buns and serve.

Grilled Tomato and Mozzarella Sandwiches

Okay, okay, we know that a grilled cheese sandwich isn't exactly the height of culinary inventions. BUT, have you had one slathered in basil-y pesto, layered with fresh tomato, and drizzled with balsamic vinaigrette? Or better yet, made in the air fryer with no need to mind the stove or scrape cheese out of your favorite pan? We didn't think so.

Serves 4

---

8 (¾- to 1-inch-thick) slices of french bread

¼ cup prepared or store-bought basil pesto

1 (8-ounce) ball mozzarella, cut into ¼-inch slices

1 large tomato, cut into ¼-inch slices

Balsamic vinaigrette or balsamic reduction, for serving (optional)

TOP 4 slices of the bread with 1 tablespoon each of the pesto. Divide the mozzarella and tomato slices between the bread slices and top each sandwich with the remaining 4 slices of bread. Arrange the sandwiches in a single layer in the air fryer, working in batches if necessary. Air fry at 330°F for 5 minutes, or until the bread is toasted and the cheese has melted completely.

DRIZZLE with the balsamic vinaigrette, if desired, slice, and serve.

Crispy Chicken Sliders

These mini sandwiches are just the thing when you're craving fast food but know you could make something just as tasty (and much healthier) at home. Thanks to a quick dip in a marinade, the chicken gets juicy and tender inside a crisp, golden crust. Then you can load up these little sandwiches with all your favorite toppings to make it a meal.

Serves 4

1 cup whole milk

2 large eggs

2 boneless, skinless chicken breasts, halved

1 cup all-purpose flour

1 cup bread crumbs

1 teaspoon ground black pepper

¼ teaspoon chili powder

Avocado or olive oil cooking spray

4 slices of provolone (optional)

4 slider buns

Your favorite slider toppings, for serving

IN a medium bowl, whisk together the milk and eggs. Add the chicken breasts and cover with plastic wrap. Refrigerate for 30 minutes or up to 1 hour.

IN a rimmed baking pan, combine the flour, bread crumbs, pepper, and chili powder and mix well. Remove the chicken pieces from the marinade and dredge them in the flour mixture so they are well coated. Arrange the chicken pieces in a single layer in the air fryer basket.

LIGHTLY coat the chicken with cooking spray and air fry at 400°F for 18 to 20 minutes, flipping halfway through. The chicken is done when an instant-read thermometer inserted in the center reads 165°F. If desired, top each piece of chicken with a piece of provolone and air fry for an additional minute to melt the cheese.

TRANSFER the chicken to the buns and serve with your favorite toppings.

Casseroles and Bakes

5

When we first started experimenting with the air fryer, we knew we wanted to create recipes that weren't just fried. Nothing against frying—there's most definitely a time and a place for it—but when you're looking to pull a meal together, sometimes you want something that doesn't make you feel like you're at a state fair. That's when we started playing around with bakes and casseroles, or layering ingredients in an oven-safe dish that fits inside the air fryer basket. The result: hits-the-spot dinners that are just as satisfying the next day for lunch. What's not to love about a cheesy, saucy, layered-with-flavor casserole packed with all manner of pasta, veggies, meat, or all of the above? These dishes make for comforting family dinners or are easily transportable anytime you need to bring something for a spread. Leftovers can be stored in an airtight container in the refrigerator for up to 4 days. To reheat, air fry in a casserole dish at 350°F for 4 to 6 minutes, until warmed through. Stir halfway through to ensure even warming.

Chicken Bacon Ranch Bake

We've taken the classic casserole base of pasta, chicken, and creamy, cheesy sauce and kicked it up a notch with the addition of zippy ranch dressing and smoky bacon. It doesn't take more effort than mixing the ingredients and popping them into the air fryer, and yet it tastes like you've put a lot of love into those layers of flavors. It's a favorite weeknight meal in both of our houses, and it makes for the BEST leftovers.

Serves 4

2½ cups penne pasta, cooked according to the package instructions and drained

2 cups cooked, shredded chicken

2 cups shredded or torn mozzarella

1 cup store-bought Alfredo sauce

1 cup Cheddar

3 slices of bacon, cooked and crumbled

3 tablespoons ranch dressing

IN a large bowl, combine the penne, chicken, 1 cup of the mozzarella, the Alfredo sauce, Cheddar, bacon, and ranch dressing. Mix well.

TRANSFER the ingredients to an 8-inch casserole or baking dish (glass or silicone). Air fry at 320°F for 8 minutes. Top the casserole with the remaining 1 cup mozzarella and cook for another 2 minutes, or until the cheese is bubbly and golden.

Buffalo Chicken Bake

Choosing a favorite casserole is like choosing your favorite child—we're really not supposed to, but if you *insist* on knowing . . . it's hard to not be a little partial to this bake. It is beyond easy to throw together (especially if you're using leftover roasted chicken or store-bought rotisserie), has all the familiar flavors of your favorite buffalo chicken dishes, and feels like a complete meal thanks to the addition of pasta. It just doesn't get better than that.

Serves 4

---

12 ounces penne pasta, cooked according to the package instructions and drained

2 cups cooked, shredded chicken

1½ cups shredded mild or medium Cheddar

4 ounces plain cream cheese, softened

½ cup buffalo sauce

¼ cup ranch dressing

IN a large bowl, combine the penne, chicken, 1 cup of the Cheddar, the cream cheese, buffalo sauce, and ranch dressing. Mix well.

TRANSFER the mixture to an 8-inch round casserole or baking dish (glass or silicone). Air fry at 320°F for 8 minutes. Top with the remaining ½ cup Cheddar and cook for another 2 to 3 minutes, until the cheese is bubbly and golden.

Chicken Alfredo Casserole

Combining the flavors of a traditional Italian Alfredo sauce with a one-pot bake makes this dish one of our favorites to reach for when it comes to weeknight dinners. Adding shredded chicken to the mix means everyone's satisfied, while plenty of gooey mozzarella ensures that this will become a staple in your meal rotation.

Serves 4

12 ounces penne pasta, cooked according to the package instructions and drained

2 cups cooked, shredded chicken

1 cup store-bought Alfredo sauce

1 cup shredded or torn mozzarella

½ cup freshly grated Parmesan

½ teaspoon minced garlic

½ teaspoon ground black pepper

2 teaspoons chopped fresh parsley

IN a large bowl, combine the penne, chicken, Alfredo sauce, ½ cup of the mozzarella, the Parmesan, garlic, and pepper. Mix well.

TRANSFER the mixture to an 8-inch round casserole or baking dish (glass or silicone). Air fry at 320°F for 6 minutes. Top with the remaining ½ cup mozzarella and cook for an additional 2 minutes, or until the cheese is bubbly and golden. Sprinkle with fresh parsley and serve.

Caprese Casserole

There's never a wrong season for a casserole, but we love how bright basil pesto, tomatoes, and fresh parsley add a little summer sunshine to this dish. It somehow manages to feel hearty and satisfying yet nice and light at the same time.

Serves 4

1 pound cooked, shredded chicken

1¼ cups shredded or torn mozzarella

1 cup cherry or grape tomatoes, halved

½ cup plus 2 tablespoons freshly grated Parmesan

¼ cup prepared or store-bought basil pesto

1 teaspoon chopped fresh parsley

IN a large bowl, combine the chicken, mozzarella, tomatoes, ½ cup of the Parmesan, and the pesto. Mix well.

TRANSFER the mixture to an 8-inch round casserole or baking dish (glass or silicone). Air fry at 320°F for 8 minutes. Top with the remaining 2 tablespoons Parmesan and the parsley. Cook for an additional 1 to 2 minutes, until the top is golden brown.

Chicken Pot Pie Casserole

When it comes to comfort food dishes, a classic, creamy, vegetable-studded chicken pot pie with buttery, flaky crust is almost always at the top of the must-have list. But between the gravy and the crust, most people don't think they have the time to make this dish unless it's a special occasion (or they're microwaving one from the freezer—no shame in that game!). That's why we made it our mission to come up with a version that delivers on every count but takes less than 20 minutes to come together. You're welcome!

Serves 4 to 6

---

1 (12-ounce) bag or 2 cups frozen mixed vegetables

⅓ cup (5 tablespoons) unsalted butter, plus ¼ cup (4 tablespoons), melted

½ cup chopped white onion

⅓ cup all-purpose flour

½ teaspoon kosher or sea salt

¼ teaspoon ground black pepper

1½ cups chicken broth

1 cup whole milk

2 cups shredded cooked chicken

1 cup panko bread crumbs

RINSE the frozen vegetables under cold running water (this will help break up any clumps of frozen veggies), drain, and set aside.

IN a large saucepan over medium heat, combine the ⅓ cup butter and the onion. Cook until the onion has softened, 2 to 3 minutes. Add the flour, salt, and pepper to the pan and whisk to incorporate into the onion, about 1 minute. While whisking, pour in the broth and milk. Whisk to ensure that there are no lumps and continue whisking until the mixture thickens and begins to bubble, about 3 minutes. Remove the pan from the heat.

FOLD the vegetables and chicken into the gravy until well incorporated. Pour the mixture into an 8-inch round casserole or baking dish (glass or silicone). It should be about three-quarters full.

IN a small bowl, mix the panko with the melted ¼ cup butter. Sprinkle the mixture evenly over the pot pie filling. Transfer the casserole dish to the air fryer basket and air fry at 350°F for 4 to 6 minutes, until the topping is golden brown. Serve warm.

Cowboy Casserole

When we think of "cowboy" anything, it's gotta be filling, flavorful, and decidedly unfussy. All of the above apply to this Tex-Mex-inspired casserole that gets a playful crunch from tater tots and rich creaminess from a secret ingredient: cream of mushroom soup. All your family or guests will know is that this is comfort food at its finest.

Serves 4

---

4 slices of bacon

½ pound ground beef

1½ cups shredded mild or medium Cheddar

½ cup canned corn kernels, drained

½ cup condensed cream of mushroom soup

½ cup sour cream

1 teaspoon onion powder

1 teaspoon ground black pepper

16 ounces frozen tater tots

LAY the bacon in a single layer in the air fryer basket and air fry at 400°F for 8 to 10 minutes, until crisp. Transfer the bacon to a paper towel–lined plate. When cool enough to handle, break up the bacon into crumbles and set aside.

WHILE the bacon cooks, brown the beef. In a large skillet over medium heat, cook the beef while breaking it up with a spoon or spatula, until it is no longer pink, 4 to 6 minutes.

IN a large bowl, combine the crumbled bacon, browned beef, 1 cup of the Cheddar, the corn, soup, sour cream, onion powder, and pepper. Mix well.

TRANSFER the mixture to an 8-inch round casserole or baking dish (glass or silicone). Evenly top the casserole with the tater tots. Air fry at 350°F for 10 to 12 minutes, until the cheese has melted and the mixture is heated through. Top the casserole with the remaining ½ cup Cheddar and cook at 320°F for 2 to 3 minutes, until the top of the casserole is golden brown.

Million-Dollar Casserole with Ritz Crackers

We love a cozy, rewarding dish at the end of a long day, ideally one that barely takes any effort to make and yet has the whole family asking for seconds. So when we developed this recipe with its rich, creamy texture punctuated with crispy, buttery Ritz crackers, you can bet that we felt like a million bucks. There's nothing fussy about this dish, but it does feel pretty . . . ritzy.

Serves 4

2½ cups cooked, shredded chicken

1 (10.75-ounce) can condensed cream of chicken soup

4 ounces plain cream cheese, softened

¼ cup sour cream

1 teaspoon garlic powder

1 sleeve of Ritz crackers, finely crushed

3 tablespoons unsalted butter, melted

IN a large bowl, combine the chicken, soup, cream cheese, sour cream, and garlic powder. Mix well. Transfer the mixture to an 8-inch round casserole or baking dish (glass or silicone) and set aside.

IN a medium bowl, combine the crushed Ritz crackers and melted butter. Mix well. Top the casserole evenly with the mixture. Air fry at 320°F for 8 to 10 minutes, until the topping is golden brown.

Bacon Cheeseburger Deluxe Casserole

This casserole is a mainstay at both of our houses. It has the flavors of a classic deluxe cheeseburger, complete with beef, cheese, ketchup, and, of course, bacon. By layering it up with pasta, this supersized, satisfying meal can do double duty as lunch throughout the week.

Serves 4 to 6

Avocado or olive oil cooking spray, or extra-virgin olive oil

4 slices of bacon

1 teaspoon extra-virgin olive oil

½ cup diced onion

1 pound lean ground beef

8 ounces elbow macaroni, cooked according to the package instructions and drained

½ cup condensed cream of mushroom soup

½ cup shredded or torn mozzarella

3 tablespoons ketchup

½ teaspoon ground black pepper

½ cup shredded Cheddar

LIGHTLY coat an 8-inch round casserole or baking dish (glass or silicone) with the cooking spray or oil. Set aside.

ARRANGE the bacon in a single layer in the air fryer basket and air fry at 400°F for 6 to 8 minutes, until crisp. Transfer the bacon to a paper towel–lined plate and set aside.

HEAT the oil in a large skillet over medium heat. When the oil shimmers, add the onion and cook, stirring occasionally, until tender, about 4 minutes. Add the beef and cook, breaking it up with a spoon or spatula, until it is no longer pink, 4 to 6 minutes. Remove the pan from the heat, then drain the excess grease from the pan and discard.

IN a large bowl, combine the beef mixture, pasta, soup, mozzarella, ketchup, and pepper. Crumble the bacon into the bowl and stir to mix well.

POUR the mixture into the prepared dish and sprinkle the Cheddar over the top. Air fry at 320°F for 5 to 6 minutes, until the cheese has melted and is golden brown. Serve hot.

Beef and Bean Taco Casserole

Consider this your new twist on Taco Tuesday! It's a flavorful casserole stuffed with all your family's favorite taco ingredients. What really puts it over the top is a sprinkling of tortilla chips, which lend great crunchy texture and classic hard-shell taco flavor.

Serves 4

½ pound ground beef

1 cup crushed tortilla chips

1 cup Mexican blend cheese

½ cup refried beans

½ cup black beans, rinsed and drained

½ cup your favorite salsa

2 tablespoons taco seasoning

1 tablespoon chopped green onion (green part only)

IN a large skillet over medium heat, cook the beef, breaking it up with a spoon or spatula, until it is no longer pink, 4 to 6 minutes. Drain the excess grease from the pan and discard.

IN a large bowl, combine the cooked ground beef, tortilla chips, ½ cup of the cheese, the refried beans, black beans, salsa, taco seasoning, and green onion. Mix well.

POUR the mixture into an 8-inch round casserole or baking dish (glass or silicone). Air fry at 320°F for 8 minutes. Top the casserole with the remaining ½ cup cheese and cook for another 2 to 3 minutes, until the cheese is melted and turning golden brown.

King Ranch Chicken Casserole

This recipe gives the air fryer treatment to an old-school recipe. Meaning it's got all the nostalgic flavors as the original but with a fraction of the cook time. We love this dish as is, but you could also kick things up a notch with a shot of your favorite hot sauce in the chicken mixture and a dollop of sour cream on top to serve.

Serves 4

---

8 (6-inch) corn tortillas, torn into bite-sized pieces

2 cups cooked, shredded chicken breast

1 cup diced tomatoes with green chiles

1 cup condensed cream of chicken soup

Your favorite hot sauce (optional)

1 cup shredded mild Cheddar

2 tablespoons chopped green onion (green part only)

Sour cream, for serving (optional)

SCATTER half of the torn tortillas over the bottom of an 8-inch round casserole or baking dish (glass or silicone).

IN a medium bowl, stir together the chicken with the tomatoes and chiles, soup, and hot sauce (if using). Add half of the chicken mixture to the baking dish and spread evenly over the tortillas. Top with ½ cup of the Cheddar, followed by the remaining tortillas, the remaining chicken mixture, and the remaining ½ cup Cheddar.

PLACE the baking dish in the air fryer basket and air fry at 320°F for 8 to 10 minutes, until the cheese is melted and golden brown. Top with the green onion and sour cream, if desired, and serve.

Chicken, Broccoli, and Rice Casserole

Chicken, broccoli, and rice have been gracing family dinner menus pretty much forever, and while they get the job done, we wanted to make things a little more interesting (and a whole lot tastier). By adding a small handful of ingredients, we've turned a serviceable dish into a downright crave-worthy one.

Serves 4

---

2 cups cooked white rice

2 cups cooked, shredded chicken

1 cup chopped broccoli florets

1 (10.5-ounce) can condensed cream of chicken soup

1 cup grated mild or medium Cheddar

¼ cup heavy cream

¼ cup chopped green onion (green part only)

¼ teaspoon kosher or sea salt

Pinch of ground black pepper

IN an 8-inch round casserole or baking dish (glass or silicone; see Note), combine the rice, chicken, broccoli, soup, ½ cup of the Cheddar, the cream, green onion, salt, and pepper. Mix well, then spread the mixture evenly over the bottom of the dish.

AIR fry at 350°F for 6 to 8 minutes, until the broccoli is tender. Sprinkle the remaining ½ cup Cheddar over the top and air fry for an additional 2 to 3 minutes, until the cheese has melted. Serve immediately.

NOTE: *You could also divide the casserole mixture between six and eight 3- to 4-inch (7-ounce) ramekins for individual servings.*

Enchilada Quinoa Casserole

Enchiladas have been around since the Aztecs brilliantly discovered the joy that is tortillas wrapped around meat and vegetables, and who are we to question a good thing?

This dish is a mainstay on our menus because of how flavorful and filling it is thanks to beans, chicken, chiles, and spices, plus our update: a semisecret serving of good-for-you quinoa. Plus, it's easier to assemble than traditional enchiladas because we've simply layered all of the filling ingredients (the best part, in our opinion) instead of having to roll individual enchiladas. You definitely won't mind having any leftovers—if you're that lucky.

Serves 4

Avocado or olive oil cooking spray, or extra-virgin olive oil

Kosher or sea salt

1 boneless, skinless chicken breast (see Note)

2 cups shredded cheese (we love a Mexican blend for this)

1 cup cooked quinoa

1 cup canned sweet corn, drained

1 cup canned black beans, drained

1 (10-ounce) can green enchilada sauce

¾ cup tomatoes with green chiles, drained

2 tablespoons plus 2 teaspoons chopped fresh cilantro leaves

½ teaspoon ground cumin

½ teaspoon chili powder

½ teaspoon ground white pepper

½ teaspoon ground black pepper

1 Roma tomato, chopped

1 small avocado, pitted, peeled, and chopped

½ cup chopped green onion (green part only)

Lime wedges, for serving (optional)

PREHEAT the air fryer to 350°F. Lightly coat an 8-inch round casserole or baking dish (glass or silicone) with oil or cooking spray and set aside.

BRING a small pot of water to a boil. Add a generous pinch of salt and add the chicken breast. Boil the chicken for 12 to 15 minutes, until an instant-read thermometer inserted in the center reads 165°F. Remove the chicken from the water and transfer to a large bowl. Use two forks to shred the chicken and set aside.

IN a medium bowl, combine 2 cups of shredded chicken with 1 cup of the cheese, plus the quinoa, corn, beans, enchilada sauce, tomatoes with chiles, 2 tablespoons of the cilantro, the cumin, chili powder, white pepper, black pepper, and salt. Mix well and transfer the mixture to the prepared baking dish.

PLACE the dish in the air fryer basket and top with the remaining 1 cup cheese. Air fry at 320°F for 8 to 10 minutes, until the cheese has melted and the casserole is heated through. Remove the baking dish from the air fryer and allow to cool for 5 minutes.

TOP the casserole with the tomato, avocado, green onion, and remaining 2 teaspoons cilantro. Serve immediately with a squeeze of lime, if desired.

NOTE: *You can also use canned chicken, rotisserie chicken, or leftover cooked chicken for this dish. You'll need about 2 cups of shredded chicken.*

Harvest Casserole with Apples, Sausage, and Sweet Potatoes

Casseroles are already one of the most heartwarming, belly-filling meals you could serve. But when you layer in autumnal flavors like sweet potatoes, apples, smoky sausage, and cranberries, you're making memories. Think of this dish when you're planning your next Thanksgiving menu—or anytime you want dinner to feel anything but ordinary.

Serves 6

1 (29-ounce) can sweet potatoes, drained

2 small or medium Granny Smith apples, cored and chopped

6 ounces smoked beef sausage, sliced

½ cup chopped yellow onion

¼ cup packed brown sugar

¼ cup dried cranberries

¼ cup slivered almonds

¼ cup (4 tablespoons) unsalted butter, melted

1 teaspoon vanilla extract

½ teaspoon kosher or sea salt

½ teaspoon ground cinnamon

IN a large bowl, combine the sweet potatoes, apples, sausage, onion, brown sugar, cranberries, almonds, butter, vanilla, salt, and cinnamon. Mix well.

TRANSFER the mixture to an 8-inch round casserole or baking dish (glass or silicone) and place it in the air fryer basket. Air fry at 300°F for 25 minutes, stirring every 5 minutes. The casserole should be lightly browned and hot. Serve warm.

Pierogi Casserole

We are always looking for new ingredients to layer into casseroles for easy weeknight meals. One day while browsing the freezer aisle at the grocery store, we spotted pierogies, which are Eastern European dumplings that come with a variety of fillings. We realized that including them in a casserole wouldn't be so different from building a stuffed pasta bake, complete with Alfredo sauce. Sure enough, it was a huge hit. It's convenience at its best, with pretty much everything going straight from the store to the air fryer.

Serves 4

10 to 12 frozen pierogis (see Note)

¾ cup store-bought Alfredo sauce

½ cup store-bought bacon crumbles

4 ounces plain cream cheese

1 cup shredded mild Cheddar

2 tablespoons chopped green onion (green part only)

ARRANGE the pierogies in a single layer in the air fryer basket. Air fry at 400°F for 10 minutes, flipping them halfway through.

TRANSFER the pierogies to an 8-inch round casserole or baking dish (glass or silicone), overlapping if needed. Top the pierogies with the Alfredo sauce, bacon, and cream cheese, followed by the Cheddar. Place the casserole dish in the air fryer basket and air fry at 320°F for 5 minutes, or until the cheese has melted and browned. Top with the green onion and serve.

NOTE: *You can find pierogis in many grocery stores in the frozen entrée aisle or in international groceries that carry goods from around the world. We especially love using pierogies with potato or onion filling.*

Southwest Chicken Casserole

We took our go-to casserole staples—chicken and cheese—and gave them a Southwest twist with black beans, corn, tomatoes, and chiles. With a melty, gooey topping plus tortilla chips for crunch, it's always a sure thing for dinner and even more exciting as lunch the next day.

Serves 4

1 cup cooked, shredded chicken

1 cup shredded mild Cheddar

½ cup corn kernels (drained, if canned)

½ cup black beans, drained and rinsed

½ cup diced tomatoes, drained

1 tablespoon diced green chiles

½ teaspoon crushed red pepper flakes

½ teaspoon ground black pepper

¾ cup tortilla chips

1 tablespoon chopped green onion (green part only)

IN a medium bowl, combine the chicken, ¼ cup of the Cheddar, the corn, beans, tomatoes, green chiles, red pepper flakes, and black pepper. Mix well.

POUR the mixture into an 8-inch round casserole or baking dish (glass or silicone) and place the dish in the air fryer basket. Air fry at 320°F for 8 minutes. Remove the air fryer basket and top the casserole with the tortilla chips, green onion, and the remaining ¾ cup Cheddar. Air fry for an additional 2 minutes, or until the cheese is melted and beginning to brown.

Meat Mains

6

When we first started Air Frying Foodie, our goal was to teach people how to use their air fryers to make family-friendly meals. So often we would see air fryer recipes for parts of meals, usually just sides, which didn't really answer that nagging, age-old question: What's for dinner? Our solution was to think about all of our favorite weeknight and special-occasion meals and then figure out how to make them work for an air fryer. The result is a chapter jam-packed with dishes that suit every mealtime, preference, and craving; deliver perfectly cooked meat and vegetables every time; and, best of all, are made with the press of a button.

Country-Style Ribs

Country-style ribs aren't actually ribs—they're cuts of pork shoulder. That means you're getting a lot more meat on the bones, and it's the same meat that you'd normally use to make pulled pork or carnitas. (Think super tender and flavorful.) You don't need to do much to these to make them a standout dish; just let the air fryer do the work before slathering 'em in sauce.

Serves 6 to 8

Avocado or olive oil cooking spray

2 pounds country-style ribs

2 teaspoons ground black pepper

1½ teaspoons garlic powder

1 teaspoon smoked paprika

½ cup your favorite barbecue sauce

PREHEAT the air fryer to 380°F. Lightly spray the air fryer basket with the cooking spray and set aside.

USE paper towels to lightly blot the ribs dry. Set aside.

IN a small bowl, combine the pepper, garlic powder, and paprika. Mix well. Evenly coat the ribs with the rub.

PLACE the ribs in a single layer in the air fryer basket. Cook at 380°F for 20 minutes. Remove the basket and brush the barbecue sauce over the tops and sides of the ribs. Return the basket to the air fryer and cook for another 2 minutes, until the internal temperature registers 145°F on an instant-read thermometer and the ribs are pull-apart tender.

Spinach Alfredo Chicken Roulades

Roulades is fancy and French for "roll-ups." More specifically, chicken breasts that have been pounded thin and stuffed with cheese and spinach, then smothered in Alfredo sauce. Believe us when we say that the only fussy thing about this dish is its name—you can have an impressive and delicious dinner on the table in no time with this simple recipe.

Serves 4

---

2 medium boneless, skinless chicken breasts (6 to 8 ounces each)

2 tablespoons prepared or store-bought basil pesto

½ teaspoon garlic powder

¼ teaspoon kosher or sea salt

Pinch of ground black pepper

½ cup shredded or torn mozzarella

¼ cup shredded or grated Parmesan

½ cup chopped or torn fresh baby spinach

3 fresh basil leaves, torn

2 large eggs

1 cup Italian-seasoned bread crumbs

Avocado or olive oil cooking spray

¾ cup Alfredo or marinara sauce, warmed (see Note)

BUTTERFLY each chicken breast, or carefully slice through the center of each breast without cutting all the way through (as though you were making a chicken "book"). Lay the butterflied chicken breasts flat between two pieces of plastic wrap or regular parchment paper, or in a large zip-top plastic bag. Use a meat mallet, rolling pin, or small pan to pound the chicken to about ¼-inch thickness.

LAY both breasts on a clean work surface. Evenly spread the pesto over each piece and season with the garlic powder, salt, and pepper. Divide the cheeses, spinach, and basil between the two breasts, covering them evenly. Tightly roll up each piece of chicken widthwise, using toothpicks to secure them.

IN a shallow dish, whisk the eggs. In a separate shallow dish, add the bread crumbs. Dredge each chicken roll-up in the whisked eggs, followed by the bread crumbs. Make sure the chicken is well coated.

LIGHTLY coat the air fryer basket with cooking spray. Set the chicken roll-ups in the basket and air fry at 380°F for 13 to 18 minutes, until the chicken is golden brown and registers 165°F on an instant-read thermometer (see Note).

DRIZZLE the Alfredo sauce (see Note) over the chicken and serve.

NOTE: *For a lighter twist, serve this with marinara sauce instead. If your chicken is on the thicker side even after pounding it thin, your cook time may be longer. Your best bet for knowing whether it's cooked through is by taking the internal temperature with an instant-read thermometer.*

Steak and Veggie Fajitas

One of the easiest ways to make everyone at the table happy is to serve a meal that can be endlessly customized to individual tastes and preferences. Fajitas are at the top of the list when we think of crowd-pleasers because so many people love flavorful, juicy steak, especially when it gets wrapped up in a tortilla and smothered in all the mixed and matched toppings you could want (think sour cream, salsa, guacamole, shredded cheese, chopped tomatoes, and fresh cilantro). Add to that the fact that the hands-on prep time is a matter of minutes, and you can see why this is a weeknight lifesaver.

Serves 4

1½ pounds flank or skirt steak, sliced into ½-inch strips

1 medium red bell pepper, seeded and sliced

1 medium green bell pepper, seeded and sliced

½ small white onion, sliced

1 tablespoon fajita seasoning mix

Lime wedges, for serving

Flour or corn tortillas, for serving

Your favorite fajita toppings, for serving

PREHEAT the air fryer to 380°F for 5 minutes.

IN a medium bowl, combine the steak, peppers, and onion. Sprinkle over the seasoning and toss until the steak and vegetables are well coated.

ADD the steak and vegetables to the air fryer basket and air fry for 18 minutes, tossing every few minutes to ensure that they are evenly cooked.

GIVE the steak and vegetables a squeeze of lime juice before serving with tortillas and toppings.

Beef and Vegetable Kebabs

The ultimate weeknight dish—or anytime dish, really—is one where the protein and vegetables can cook at the same time, ideally very quickly, and yield a flavorful complete meal. With this recipe, well, mission accomplished. And because you can stretch one steak for four people, it's budget-friendly, too.

Serves 4

1 teaspoon smoked paprika

1 teaspoon ground black pepper

1 teaspoon onion powder

½ teaspoon ground cumin

1 (8-ounce) rib eye steak, cut into 1½-inch cubes

1 small zucchini, cut into ½-inch-thick slices

1 small yellow squash, cut into ½-inch-thick slices

1 small red onion, sliced

1 medium red bell pepper, seeded and chopped into 1-inch squares

1 cup button mushrooms

Avocado or olive oil cooking spray

ON a plate or in a wide bowl, combine the paprika, black pepper, onion powder, and cumin. Set aside.

THREAD the steak and vegetables onto metal or wooden skewers (see Note) in any combination or pattern you like. Lightly coat the skewers with the cooking spray and evenly coat them with the seasoning mixture.

ARRANGE the skewers in the air fryer basket in a single layer and air fry at 350°F for 10 minutes, flipping the skewers halfway through. The vegetables should be lightly golden, and the meat should be browned. Transfer to a plate and serve.

NOTE: *If you are using wooden skewers, be sure to soak them for 20 minutes before assembling the kebabs to prevent burning.*

Chicken Wings

The secret to making these fan-favorite restaurant-quality wings at home—besides using an air fryer, of course!—is to first toss them in a little baking powder along with the seasonings. This simple trick gets you that crispy skin you're going for, which helps all that tasty sauce cling to the wings. Serve these with your game-time spread or your favorite sides.

Makes 24 wings

Avocado or olive oil cooking spray (optional)

12 chicken wings separated into pieces (24 total)

1 tablespoon extra-virgin olive oil

1 teaspoon baking powder

1 teaspoon garlic powder

½ teaspoon kosher salt

1 teaspoon ground black pepper

1 cup buffalo hot sauce or your favorite sauce

PREHEAT the air fryer to 380°F. Lightly spray the air fryer basket with cooking spray or line with air fryer parchment paper. Set aside.

IN a large bowl, combine the chicken wings with the oil, baking powder, garlic powder, salt, and pepper. Mix well.

ARRANGE the wings in a single layer in the air fryer basket. Cook for 20 minutes, flipping the wings every 5 minutes. Increase the temperature to 400°F and cook for an additional 2 minutes for extra-crispy skin. The meat should register 165°F on an instant-read thermometer.

TRANSFER the wings to a large bowl and toss with the sauce. Serve hot.

Southern Fried Chicken

Sometimes you shouldn't mess with a good thing, and this is one of them. Chicken drumsticks brined in buttermilk and seasoned with a cayenne kick will forever be the gold standard of fried chicken, and for that reason, we're letting it ride. Though with one key difference: no need to deal with a big pan of hot oil!

Serves 4

---

1 tablespoon extra-virgin olive oil, plus more for greasing

4 bone-in chicken drumsticks

1 cup buttermilk

1 cup bread crumbs

2 tablespoons all-purpose flour

1 teaspoon baking powder

1 teaspoon paprika

½ teaspoon onion powder

¼ teaspoon cayenne pepper

¼ teaspoon ground black pepper

LIGHTLY coat the air fryer basket with oil. Set aside.

PAT the chicken dry with a paper towel. Brush the drumsticks with the oil on all sides. Add the buttermilk to a shallow dish or container that will fit all of the drumsticks, and arrange them in the buttermilk. Let them soak in the refrigerator for 30 minutes, flipping them halfway through if they're not submerged.

IN a medium bowl, stir together the bread crumbs, flour, baking powder, paprika, onion powder, cayenne, and black pepper. Remove the chicken from the buttermilk, then dip each piece in the bread crumb mixture until well coated.

ARRANGE the drumsticks in the air fryer basket in a single layer. Air fry at 400°F for 20 minutes, rotating the chicken halfway through. An instant-read thermometer inserted in the thickest part of the chicken should register 165°F. Serve hot.

Kung Pao Chicken

When we're looking for inspiration for new dishes, one of the first places we go back to is the take-out menu. This popular dish, which is pretty much a given in many Chinese restaurants here in the United States, is surprisingly simple to make at home. And not just that; it's simple to re-create its signature layers of aromatic- and chili-packed flavor and texture. (Thanks to an assist from store-bought kung pao sauce.)

Serves 4

---

1 pound boneless, skinless chicken breast or thighs, cut into 1- to 2-inch pieces

1 medium red bell pepper, seeded and cut into 1-inch strips

1 medium green bell pepper, seeded and cut into 1-inch strips

1 cup store-bought kung pao sauce

1 teaspoon crushed red pepper flakes

½ cup unsalted roasted cashews or dry roasted peanuts

¼ cup chopped green onion (green part only)

Cooked white rice or noodles (we like Asian noodles, such as lo mein egg noodles), for serving

---

IN a medium shallow dish or a gallon-size plastic zip-top bag, combine the chicken and bell peppers with ½ cup of the kung pao sauce and the red pepper flakes. Let the chicken marinate in the refrigerator for 30 minutes.

TRANSFER the chicken mixture plus the marinade to the air fryer basket and air fry at 380°F for 10 minutes. Use tongs or a fork to toss the mixture, then air fry for another 5 minutes. The chicken should be completely cooked through and the bell peppers very tender.

TOP the mixture in the basket with the remaining ½ cup kung pao sauce, the nuts, and green onion. Toss together and air fry for another 2 to 3 minutes, until warmed through. Serve over rice or noodles.

Filet and Mushrooms

One of the things the Air Frying Foodie community loves most, and which makes our recipes stand out from other air frying blogs and sites, is a recipe for a complete meal. We get it—it doesn't get any easier or more satisfying than adding your ingredients to an air fryer basket and ending up with a cooked-to-your-liking protein and veg that can go straight to the table. But what really makes this dish a fan favorite is the rich, earthy, meaty combo of mushrooms and steak.

Serves 2

FOR THE STEAK

2 (4- to 6-ounce) filet mignon steaks, at room temperature for 30 minutes

1 tablespoon extra-virgin olive oil

½ teaspoon kosher or sea salt

½ teaspoon ground black pepper

FOR THE MUSHROOMS

16 ounces portobello mushrooms, rubbed clean with a damp cloth

3 tablespoons extra-virgin olive oil

1 garlic clove, minced, or 1 tablespoon garlic powder

½ teaspoon kosher salt

¼ teaspoon ground black pepper

PREP THE STEAKS: Pat the steaks dry with paper towels and coat them with the oil. Season with the salt and pepper and arrange the steaks in a single layer on one side of the air fryer basket. Set aside.

PREP THE MUSHROOMS: In a medium bowl, toss the mushrooms with the oil to coat. Add the garlic, salt, and pepper and toss again until the mushrooms are evenly seasoned. Transfer the mushrooms to the other side of the air fryer basket.

AIR fry at 380°F for 10 to 12 minutes, flipping halfway through and removing the mushrooms when they are fork-tender. If needed, allow the mushrooms to continue cooking for another 2 to 4 minutes. Check the internal temperature of the steaks to make sure they're done to your liking (see Note).

FOR extra juicy, tender steaks, let the meat rest for 5 to 10 minutes before serving with the mushrooms.

NOTE: *We recommend taking the internal temperature of your steak with an instant-read thermometer to make sure it's cooked exactly to your liking. As a baseline, we call for cooking the steaks for 6 minutes per side for medium doneness (which may vary based on the size and wattage of your air fryer). Here is an at-a-glance list of degrees of doneness and corresponding temps: rare (125°F), medium-rare (135°F), medium (145°F), medium-well (155°F), well done (160°F).*

Beef Stroganoff

This is one of those old-school dishes that we grew up eating that still reminds us of talking about the day's events over dinner. The combination of earthy mushrooms and cream of mushroom soup plus beef and a kick of Worcestershire sauce tastes like it took hours to develop that kind of flavor, and yet you could easily make this cozy, comforting dish on a weeknight. Serve this over a bed of egg noodles for a meal that will fill the hungriest of bellies.

Serves 4

1 pound stir-fry beef, tenderloin, or sirloin, cut into thin strips

1 small yellow onion, sliced

1 cup sliced portobello mushrooms

1 tablespoon extra-virgin olive oil

1 tablespoon Worcestershire sauce

1 teaspoon garlic powder

½ teaspoon sea salt

¼ teaspoon ground black pepper

1 cup condensed cream of mushroom soup

¼ cup beef broth (low-sodium or regular)

¼ cup sour cream

1 (16-ounce) package egg noodles, cooked according to the package instructions and drained

IN a large bowl, combine the beef, onion, mushrooms, and oil and toss to coat. Add the Worcestershire, garlic powder, salt, and pepper and toss again. Place the mixture in the air fryer basket and air fry at 380°F for 6 to 8 minutes, tossing halfway through cooking. The beef should be cooked through and register 145°F on an instant-read thermometer.

TRANSFER the mixture to an 8-inch round casserole or baking dish (glass or silicone). Stir in the soup, broth, and sour cream. Place the casserole dish in the air fryer basket and air fry at 380°F for 2 to 3 minutes, until warmed through. Serve over egg noodles.

Parmesan-Breaded Pork Chops

Pork chops are one of the easiest cuts of meat to cook—and one of the easiest to *over*cook. We've removed all of the guesswork by first dredging them in breading that's been kicked up a notch with salty Parmesan, then popping them into the air fryer instead of messing around with an oily pan. It's a guaranteed winner that just needs a simple side from chapter 9 to be the perfect meal.

Serves 4

Avocado or olive oil cooking spray, or extra-virgin olive oil

1 cup panko bread crumbs

¼ cup shredded or grated Parmesan

1 tablespoon dried parsley flakes

½ teaspoon sea salt

¼ teaspoon ground black pepper

½ cup all-purpose flour

1 large egg, beaten

4 (¼-inch-thick) boneless pork chops

LIGHTLY coat the air fryer basket with the cooking spray or oil. Set aside.

IN a shallow bowl, combine the panko, Parmesan, parsley flakes, salt, and pepper. In another shallow bowl, add the flour. And in a third, add the egg.

TOSS a pork chop in the flour, coating both sides. Next, dredge the pork chop in the egg, and finally, coat with the panko mixture. Place the pork chop in the air fryer basket and repeat with the remaining pork chops.

AIR fry at 400°F for 10 to 12 minutes, making sure the pork chops are not overlapping, flipping halfway through. The bread crumb coating should be golden brown and crispy, and an instant-read thermometer should read 145°F when inserted in the center of a pork chop.

Chicken Drumsticks

Did you ever think you'd be able to have a delicious BBQ chicken dinner in less than 20 minutes? By using the drumsticks, you're not only guaranteeing flavorful, juicy meat, but you're also cutting the cook time way down, though the simple combination of barbecue sauce, brown sugar, and garlic powder makes it taste like these spent hours in the smoker. It's a classic recipe that instantly gained a dedicated following among our readers.

Serves 2 to 4

Avocado or olive oil cooking spray, or extra-virgin olive oil

6 skin-on, bone-in chicken drumsticks

2 tablespoons packed brown sugar

1 teaspoon garlic powder

½ cup your favorite barbecue sauce, warmed

LIGHTLY coat the air fryer basket with the cooking spray or oil. Place the chicken in a single layer in the basket. Set aside.

IN a small bowl, mix together the brown sugar and garlic powder. Sprinkle the spice mix over the chicken, making sure to coat each piece well on both sides. It can help to gently pat the mix into the meat to help it stick.

AIR fry at 400°F for 20 minutes, flipping halfway through. The chicken is done when an instant-read thermometer inserted in the thickest part of the drumstick reads 165°F.

TRANSFER the chicken to a plate and brush each piece all over with the barbecue sauce. Serve immediately.

Honey-Glazed Beef Skewers

Soy sauce and honey are the secret ingredients for these sticky-sweet yet savory skewers. With just a handful of ingredients (and minutes), you'll have an impressively flavorful main that's as delicious as it is fun to eat. And yet, as distinctive as they are, they're really versatile when it comes to assembling a meal. We can't think of a single side that wouldn't go well with juicy pieces of perfectly cooked steak.

Serves 4

---

1 pound top sirloin steak

¼ cup plus 2 tablespoons honey

¼ cup soy sauce

1 tablespoon sesame oil

1 teaspoon minced garlic (about 2 medium cloves)

1 teaspoon grated fresh ginger

Avocado or olive oil cooking spray (optional)

SLICE sirloin into ¼-inch strips roughly 6 to 8 inches in length. Thread the steak pieces onto metal or wooden skewers (see Note) lengthwise. Set aside.

IN a shallow bowl or large plastic zip-top bag, combine ¼ cup of the honey plus the soy sauce, sesame oil, garlic, and ginger. Transfer 2 tablespoons of the sauce to a small bowl and set aside. Add the skewers to the remaining sauce and coat well. Allow the meat to marinate at room temperature for 30 minutes.

LIGHTLY coat the air fryer basket with cooking spray or line it with air fryer parchment paper. Transfer the skewers to the basket and air fry at 400°F for 6 to 8 minutes. The meat should be browned.

WHILE the skewers cook, make the glaze. In a small bowl, combine the remaining 2 tablespoons honey with the reserved 2 tablespoons marinade. Once the skewers have finished cooking, brush them with the glaze to coat. Serve immediately.

NOTE: *If you are using wooden skewers, be sure to soak them in water for 20 minutes before assembling to prevent burning.*

Lamb Chops

Cooking lamb chops in the air fryer is the easiest way to have a "gourmet" meal with none of the fuss (or dishes). Lamb is already super flavorful on its own, but the addition of fresh rosemary and thyme plus garlic is what takes this from "Great homemade meal" to "Where did you pick this up from?" You don't need more than a simple side of veg to make these feel like a special (yet effortless) meal.

Serves 4

---

1 (2-pound) rack of lamb or 8 precut lamb chops

2 tablespoons extra-virgin olive oil

2 teaspoons chopped fresh rosemary leaves (1 to 2 sprigs)

1 teaspoon fresh thyme leaves (1 to 2 sprigs)

1 teaspoon minced garlic (about 2 medium cloves)

½ teaspoon sea salt

½ teaspoon ground black pepper

IF you are using a rack of lamb, cut with the grain to separate the chops. Set aside.

IN a medium bowl, combine the oil, rosemary, thyme, garlic, salt, and pepper. Mix well. Working in batches, add the lamb chops to the oil and herb mixture and toss to coat. Place the coated lamb chops in the air fryer basket in a single layer. You may need to do this in batches as well.

AIR fry at 380°F for 10 to 12 minutes, until an instant-read thermometer reads 145°F. Let the chops rest for 3 to 5 minutes before serving.

Stuffed Bell Peppers

This dish is the best of both worlds: It's (quite literally) packed with flavor, and yet it's incredibly convenient. We'll reach for these savory, hearty peppers if we need to whip up something quick for dinner, or we'll add them to our lunch rotation for the week and make a batch as part of meal prep. No matter which meal you enjoy them for, they're going to make you feel full and satisfied without weighing you down.

Serves 4

4 bell peppers (any color)

1 teaspoon extra-virgin olive oil

1 small white onion, diced

1 teaspoon minced garlic

1 cup tomato sauce

1 tablespoon Italian seasoning

1 pound cooked fajita-spiced shredded chicken

2 cups cooked white rice

2 cups shredded Colby Jack

1 tablespoon chopped fresh flat-leaf parsley

PREPARE the peppers by slicing them in half lengthwise and using a spoon to carefully scoop out the seeds and white membrane. Set aside.

HEAT the oil in a medium saucepan over medium-high heat. Add the onion and garlic and cook, stirring, until slightly softened, about 2 minutes. Stir in the tomato sauce and Italian seasoning and remove the pan from the heat. Add the chicken and rice to the pan and stir until just combined.

DIVIDE the stuffing between the prepared peppers. Arrange the peppers in a single layer in the air fryer basket and air fry at 360°F for 10 minutes. Top the peppers with the cheese and cook for 2 to 3 more minutes, until the cheese has melted. Sprinkle with the parsley and serve.

Beef and Vegetable Pie

We took a traditional British dish and put our Air Frying Foodie spin on it. For starters, we packed a ton of flavor into a thick, creamy gravy that gets studded with vegetables and cubed beef. Then we gave you permission to use store-bought crust to drape over the "pie," shaving tons of time off prep. But the best part is that in under 20 minutes, this dish bakes up into a showstopping entrée that's still comfort food at heart.

Serves 6

1 pound cubed beef

⅓ cup (5 tablespoons) unsalted butter

½ medium yellow or white onion, sliced

⅓ cup all-purpose flour

1½ cups beef broth (low-sodium or regular)

1 cup whole milk

1 teaspoon garlic powder

1 teaspoon sea salt

½ teaspoon ground black pepper

1 (12-ounce) bag frozen peas and carrots

1 refrigerated pie crust

IN a large skillet over medium heat, cook the meat until browned on all sides, 4 to 6 minutes. Set aside.

HEAT the butter in a large saucepan over medium heat. Add the onion and cook until softened, 1 to 2 minutes. Stir in the flour and cook until thickened, about 1 minute. Add the broth, milk, garlic powder, salt, and pepper and stir until the mixture begins to bubble and thicken, 3 to 4 minutes. Remove the pan from the heat.

STIR the beef and vegetables into the gravy and pour the mixture in an 8-inch round casserole or baking dish (glass or silicone). Use a rolling pin to roll the pie crust to ⅛-inch thickness. Carefully transfer the crust to the top of the casserole dish and trim the edges. Cut 1-inch vents in the dough with a knife, or pierce 4 to 5 times with a fork for venting.

TRANSFER the casserole dish to the air fryer basket and cook at 350°F for 13 to 15 minutes, until the crust is golden brown and crisp.

Spice-Rubbed Pork Tenderloin

If you fall in love with this dish at first bite, you won't be alone in that. Thousands of our followers have named this as their favorite dish, and it's easy to see why! It is amazing how juicy pork tenderloin can be when it's seasoned with a sweet-salty rub with a hint of heat. Add any one of the sides from chapter 9, and you'll have a back-pocket meal that's perfect for weeknights or for when you want to serve a dinner that feels a little more special.

Serves 4

---

1 (1¼- to 1½-pound) pork tenderloin

2 tablespoons packed brown sugar

½ teaspoon sea salt

½ teaspoon paprika

½ teaspoon garlic powder

¼ teaspoon ground black pepper

¼ teaspoon chili powder or cayenne pepper

1 tablespoon extra-virgin olive oil

1 tablespoon dried parsley flakes

PAT the tenderloin dry with a paper towel. Using a sharp knife, trim away any larger pieces of fat and discard. Set aside.

IN a small bowl, combine the brown sugar, salt, paprika, garlic powder, black pepper, and chili powder or cayenne. Mix well.

COAT the tenderloin completely with the oil, then sprinkle the spice mixture over the tenderloin and use your hands to spread it so the meat is evenly coated.

PLACE the tenderloin in the air fryer basket or tray and air fry at 400°F for 20 to 22 minutes, turning halfway through. The meat is done when the center registers 145°F on an instant-read thermometer. Transfer the tenderloin to a plate or cutting board and allow the meat to rest for 8 to 10 minutes before slicing and serving. Sprinkle with the dried parsley and enjoy.

STORE any leftovers in an airtight container in the refrigerator for up to 4 days.

Teriyaki Pork Kebabs

Kebabs are one of the best dinner hacks—they take minutes to prep (not including the hands-off time to let them soak up a tasty teriyaki marinade), and they automatically include a protein and lots of veggies. Plus, they're fun to eat. There's something about nibbling your meal off a skewer that gets even the pickiest eaters excited. These are also easily customizable, so feel free to leave out or double up on any of the ingredients, depending on your and your family's preferences.

Serves 4

---

1 pound boneless pork loin, cut into 1-inch cubes

8 ounces small portobello mushrooms

1 medium red bell pepper, seeded and chopped into 1-inch squares

1 medium green bell pepper, seeded and chopped into 1-inch squares

½ medium red onion, sliced into wedges

½ cup fresh pineapple chunks

1 cup Homemade Teriyaki Sauce (page 56) or store-bought

THREAD 4 metal or wooden skewers (see Note) with an assortment of the pork, mushrooms, peppers, onion, and pineapple.

IN a shallow bowl or large plastic zip-top bag, combine ½ cup of the teriyaki sauce with the skewers. Make sure the skewers are well coated with the sauce and marinate for at least 1 hour or up to overnight. (Be sure to put them in the fridge if marinating them for longer than 1 hour.)

PLACE the skewers in the air fryer basket in a single layer. Brush a light coating of the marinade over each skewer and air fry at 370°F for 13 to 15 minutes, until an instant-read thermometer inserted in the center of one of the pork cubes registers 145°F.

DRIZZLE the remaining ½ cup teriyaki sauce over the skewers and serve immediately.

NOTE: *If you are using wooden skewers, be sure to soak them for 20 minutes before assembling the kebabs to prevent burning.*

Chicken-Fried Steak

You say greasy-spoon classic, we say the perfect weeknight meal thanks to no deep-frying. And yet, this version is nothing less than 100 percent authentic comfort food. A side of Scalloped Red Potatoes (page 193) or Green Bean Casserole (page 194) would make it feel like you were eating out at your favorite diner.

Serves 4

Avocado or olive oil cooking spray

1½ cups all-purpose flour

2 teaspoons baking powder

1 teaspoon ground black pepper

½ teaspoon paprika

½ teaspoon onion powder

½ teaspoon garlic powder

1 cup whole milk

2 large eggs, beaten

1 tablespoon Tabasco, Louisiana Hot Sauce, or your favorite hot sauce

4 (4- to 6-ounce) cube steaks

LIGHTLY spray the air fryer basket with cooking spray or line with air fryer parchment paper. Set aside.

IN a large shallow bowl, combine the flour, baking powder, pepper, paprika, onion powder, and garlic powder. Mix well. In a second large shallow bowl, combine the milk, eggs, and hot sauce. Mix well.

DIP the cube steaks into the flour mixture to coat well. Shake off any excess, then dip them into the milk mixture. Let any excess drip off, and lay the steaks on a baking sheet.

SPRAY both sides of the steaks with a light spritz of the cooking spray. Arrange the steaks in a single layer in the air fryer basket and cook at 400°F for 8 minutes. Use a spatula to carefully flip each steak, spray once more with the cooking spray, and cook for another 5 to 6 minutes, until the tops are golden brown with a crispy coating and the internal temperature reads 135° to 145°F on an instant-read thermometer (for medium to medium-well).

STORE leftovers in an airtight container in the refrigerator for up to 3 days.

Cornish Game Hens

Cornish game hens might seem like some fussy dish you only see on restaurant menus, but when you consider that they're really just mini chickens that cook up in no time, we hope you'll give 'em a chance! Or maybe you'll be sold when we tell you about the herbed butter these get slathered with before they get cooked to juicy-on-the-inside, crisp-on-the-outside perfection. It makes a great family night dish or a dinner party main course.

Serves 4

---

2 (1- to 2-pound) Cornish game hens

2 tablespoons unsalted butter, melted

½ teaspoon kosher salt

¼ teaspoon ground black pepper

½ teaspoon dried thyme

½ teaspoon dried rosemary

½ teaspoon dried sage

USE a paper towel to lightly blot dry the game hens. Set aside.

IN a small bowl, combine the melted butter with the salt, pepper, thyme, rosemary, and sage.

BRUSH the mixture over both hens, making sure they're well coated. Place the hens in the air fryer basket, breast side down. Air fry at 350°F for 15 minutes, then flip the hens breast side up. Cook for another 15 minutes, or until the hens are golden brown and the internal temperature registers 165°F on an instant-read thermometer.

Chicken Parmesan

Normally, making chicken Parmesan takes a pretty big investment of time—getting the chicken nice and crispy, developing flavor in the sauce, layering it all up with cheese, and baking it until it's good and melty. So you can imagine our surprise when we figured out we could accomplish all those things . . . in 10 minutes. Your family will never be able to tell the difference, except for the extra time you now have to spend with them.

Serves 4

---

2 (8-ounce) boneless, skinless chicken breasts, halved

½ cup bread crumbs

½ cup panko bread crumbs

2 tablespoons Italian seasoning

2 large eggs, beaten

½ cup freshly grated Parmesan

¼ cup shredded mozzarella

¼ cup store-bought or homemade marinara sauce

PREHEAT the air fryer to 350°F.

PLACE the chicken breast pieces on a piece of regular parchment paper or plastic wrap. Place another piece on top. Use a meat tenderizer or rolling pin to pound the chicken breasts until they are ½ to ¾ inch thick. Set aside.

IN a medium bowl, combine the bread crumbs, panko, and Italian seasoning. Mix well. Place the beaten eggs in another medium bowl.

DIP each piece of chicken into the eggs to coat well. Let any excess drip off, then dip the chicken into the bread crumb mixture to coat well. Place the coated chicken breasts in a single layer in the air fryer basket.

IN a small bowl, combine the Parmesan and mozzarella. Set aside.

COOK the chicken at 350°F for 7 minutes. Top each piece of chicken with 1 tablespoon of the marinara and 1 to 3 tablespoons of the cheese (depending on the size of your chicken and how cheesy you'd like it). Cook for an additional 5 minutes, until the chicken is golden brown and the cheese has melted.

STORE any leftovers in an airtight container in the refrigerator for up to 3 days. Reheat in the air fryer on 350°F for 2 minutes, or until the chicken is warmed through.

NOTE: *We love serving this dish with a side of noodles (spaghetti, fettuccine, zucchini) or roasted vegetables. Add a sprinkle of chopped, fresh parsley before serving. And definitely don't skip making chicken Parm sandwiches with the leftovers!*

Chicken with Mixed Veggies

This may not be the flashiest dish in the book, but that doesn't make it any less beloved. It's just one of those workhorse recipes that checks all the right boxes: It hits the spot for dinner every time, pleases just about everyone, and is great for prepping ahead. Plus, you change up how you're serving it, so it never gets boring. We like scooping the chicken and vegetables over rice or wrapping everything up in a tortilla.

Serves 4

---

1 teaspoon garlic powder

1 teaspoon onion powder

1 teaspoon ground black pepper

½ teaspoon smoked paprika

1 pound boneless, skinless chicken breast, cut into 1-inch cubes

1 cup sliced bell pepper (red, green, or yellow)

1 cup sliced zucchini

½ cup chopped red onion

1½ tablespoons extra-virgin olive oil

2 tablespoons chopped fresh parsley

PREHEAT the air fryer to 400°F.

IN a small bowl, combine the garlic powder, onion powder, black pepper, and paprika. Mix well.

IN a medium bowl, toss the chicken, bell pepper, zucchini, and onion with the oil until well coated. Add the seasoning mixture and toss to coat the chicken and vegetables.

TRANSFER the mixture to the air fryer basket and air fry at 400°F for 10 minutes, shaking the basket halfway through. The chicken should be lightly golden and have no pink in the center, and the vegetables should be hot. Sprinkle with the fresh parsley and serve.

Creamy Pesto Chicken

We think store-bought pesto sauce is one of the greatest pantry staples you can have on hand because of how it instantly adds fresh, bright flavor to just about anything. One way to make it really special, though, is to fold it into a homemade cream sauce. It's the kind of rich, creamy goodness that elevates the simplest of dishes, whether it's chicken breasts, pasta, or both.

Serves 4

1 pound boneless, skinless chicken breasts, halved, or 4 (4-ounce) breasts

2 tablespoons plus 1 teaspoon prepared or store-bought pesto

1 teaspoon minced garlic

1½ cups heavy cream

1 tablespoon all-purpose flour

½ teaspoon sea salt

2 tablespoons shredded or grated Parmesan

BRUSH both sides of each piece of chicken breast with 1 teaspoon of the pesto and arrange the pieces in a single layer in the air fryer basket. Air fry at 380°F for 8 minutes, then turn the chicken. Cook for another 7 to 10 minutes, until the chicken is golden and an instant-read thermometer registers 165°F when inserted in the center.

WHILE the chicken cooks, make the creamy pesto sauce. In a small saucepan over low heat, combine the remaining 1 tablespoon pesto with the garlic. Cook for 1 minute to infuse the garlic flavor, then stir in the cream, flour, and salt. Increase the heat to medium and cook, while stirring, until the sauce begins to simmer, about 5 minutes. Remove the pot from the heat and immediately stir in the Parmesan until it melts into the sauce.

POUR as much sauce as you like over the chicken and serve immediately.

NOTE: *You will end up with 2 cups of creamy pesto sauce, which is more than you'll need, but leftover sauce can be stored in an airtight container or jar in the refrigerator for 5 to 7 days. This recipe calls for spooning the sauce over portions of chicken breast, but we also recommend slicing the cooked chicken into bite-sized pieces and tossing them with pasta and a generous dollop of sauce. Or toss the sauce with plain pasta and call it dinner!*

Sweet and Sour Pork Stir-Fry

The combination of pork and sweet pineapple cooked until crispy, juicy, and saucy and spooned over rice is pretty much a sell on its own. The fact that you can make this dish in under 15 minutes is, well, just gravy. If you're like us, you'll definitely find yourself reaching for this recipe on a regular basis.

Serves 4

¾ cup bread crumbs

1 tablespoon minced garlic

½ teaspoon sea salt

½ teaspoon ground black pepper

1 pound pork tenderloin, cut into 1-inch pieces

2 tablespoons soy sauce

½ cup diced pineapple

1 red bell pepper, seeded and sliced

3 green onions, sliced (green part only)

Avocado or olive oil cooking spray

2 cups rice, cooked according to the package instructions

IN a large bowl, stir together the bread crumbs, garlic, salt, and black pepper. Set aside.

IN a medium bowl, combine the pork and soy sauce and toss to coat. Add the pork to the bread crumb mixture and toss until well coated.

TRANSFER the pork to the air fryer basket along with the pineapple, bell pepper, and green onions. Lightly coat everything with the cooking spray and toss to combine. Air fry at 380°F for 10 minutes, tossing halfway through, or until an instant-read thermometer inserted in the pork registers 160°F.

POUR the mixture over the rice and serve.

Maple-Glazed Pork Chops with Brussels Sprouts

There's a lot to love about this recipe: Most of the preparation is hands-off, the maple glaze gives the pork tons of flavor that complements the meat's natural sweetness, and when combined with the crispy, Parmesan-crusted brussels sprouts, it's a complete and satisfying meal. This is a great dish for feeding the family during the week or for serving to guests for a nicer get-together.

Serves 4

FOR THE MAPLE-GLAZED PORK CHOPS

¼ cup maple syrup

1 tablespoon honey mustard

1 teaspoon minced garlic

½ teaspoon paprika

½ teaspoon sea salt

¼ teaspoon ground black pepper

4 (6-ounce, ½-inch-thick) boneless pork chops

FOR THE BRUSSELS SPROUTS

1 pound brussels sprouts, trimmed, halved, and rinsed

1 tablespoon extra-virgin olive oil

2 cloves garlic, pressed or minced

¼ teaspoon sea salt

Pinch of ground black pepper

¼ cup shredded or grated Parmesan

MAKE the maple-glazed pork chops: In a shallow bowl, stir together the maple syrup, honey mustard, garlic, paprika, salt, and pepper. Add the pork chops and toss until coated with the glaze. Cover with plastic wrap and refrigerate for at least 2 hours and up to 4.

REMOVE the pork chops from the glaze and arrange them in the basket of the air fryer in a single layer. Air fry at 400°F for 9 to 11 minutes, until an instant-read thermometer inserted in the center of a pork chop registers 145°F. Remove the pork chops from the air fryer and cover with foil while you make the brussels sprouts.

MAKE the brussels sprouts: In a large bowl, combine the brussels sprouts with the oil and garlic. Toss to coat the sprouts well. Sprinkle with the salt and pepper and toss again to coat.

SPREAD the brussels sprouts over the bottom of the air fryer basket. Air fry at 400°F for 10 to 12 minutes, until the sprouts are tender and beginning to brown. Sprinkle the Parmesan over the top and air fry for another 1 to 2 minutes, until the cheese melts.

SERVE alongside the pork chops.

Pork Chops with Apple Stuffing

We often reach for pork chops when developing new recipes because they're such a great blank canvas and pair well with just about any flavors. We also love how easy it is to stuff a pork chop, which is not only a great way to keep the meat moist but also makes for a more exciting meal. The buttery breaded apples and craisins transform what is a truly simple dish into an elegant-feeling main course.

Serves 2 (see Note)

1 Granny Smith apple, peeled, cored, and diced

1 cup Italian-seasoned bread crumbs

⅓ cup craisins

¼ cup (4 tablespoons) unsalted butter, cut into small pieces

2 (6-ounce, 1-inch-thick) boneless pork chops

Avocado or olive oil cooking spray

½ teaspoon ground black pepper

¼ teaspoon garlic powder

IN a medium bowl, combine the apple, bread crumbs, craisins, and butter. Mix well.

USE a sharp knife to cut into the side of each pork chop about halfway through, creating a roughly 3-inch-wide "pocket." Stuff each pork chop with the apple mixture. Add the pork chops to the air fryer basket and lightly coat the tops with cooking spray. Season the pork chops with ¼ teaspoon of the pepper and ⅛ teaspoon of the garlic powder.

AIR fry at 330°F for 12 minutes. Carefully flip the pork chops and spray again with the cooking spray. Season with the remaining ¼ teaspoon pepper and ⅛ teaspoon garlic powder. Air fry for another 12 minutes, until an instant-read thermometer inserted in the center of a pork chop registers 145°F. Serve hot.

NOTE: *This recipe can easily be doubled to serve 4.*

Rib Eye and Asparagus

One of the most satisfying things about cooking at home is that you can re-create dishes you love ordering in a restaurant—and make them *exactly* the way you like them. Which is why when we taught our followers how to make perfectly cooked, perfectly seasoned rib eye steaks, the recipe instantly became a fan favorite. Paired with fresh, tender asparagus, it's a steak house–worthy meal in the comfort of your own dining room.

Serves 2

FOR THE RIB EYE STEAKS
2 (16-ounce) rib eye steaks
1 tablespoon extra-virgin olive oil
½ teaspoon sea salt
½ teaspoon ground black pepper

FOR THE ASPARAGUS
1 pound asparagus
1 tablespoon extra-virgin olive oil
⅛ teaspoon sea salt
⅛ teaspoon ground black pepper

MAKE the rib eye steaks: Take the steaks out of the refrigerator 1 hour before cooking. Preheat the air fryer to 400°F.

WHEN ready to cook, coat the steaks with the oil and season on all sides with the salt and pepper. Place the steaks in the air fryer basket and air fry at 400°F for 6 to 8 minutes, until the first side has a good crust. Flip the steaks and air fry for another 6 to 8 minutes, until the steaks are done to your preference (125°F for rare, 135°F for medium-rare, 145°F for medium, 155°F for medium-well, and 160°F for well done).

TRANSFER the steaks to a plate along with any juices in the bottom of the air fryer. Let the steaks rest for 5 to 10 minutes before serving.

MEANWHILE, make the asparagus: Rinse the asparagus under cold running water and pat dry. Trim the fibrous ends off of the asparagus. An easy way to do this is to bend each spear an inch or two from the bottom; they'll snap in the right spot.

BRUSH the asparagus with the oil and sprinkle with the salt and pepper. Arrange the asparagus in a single layer in the air fryer basket and air fry at 400°F for 8 to 10 minutes, until tender to your liking.

Spicy Beef Stir-Fry

This homemade version of the popular Chinese take-out dish gives anything you could have delivered a run for its money. The steak gets a sweet-savory treatment from an easy soy sauce and brown sugar marinade, which really brings the heat thanks to spices and fresh ginger. The meat gets nice and caramelized as it cooks up alongside bell peppers and snow peas—and in less time than it would take you to pick up your order.

Serves 4

¼ cup soy sauce

¼ cup packed brown sugar

1 tablespoon sesame oil

1 teaspoon chili powder

1 teaspoon crushed red pepper flakes

1 teaspoon grated fresh ginger

1 pound flank steak, cut into ⅛-inch-thick strips

1 red bell pepper, seeded and sliced thin

1 yellow bell pepper, seeded and sliced thin

1 cup fresh snow peas

1 teaspoon sesame seeds (optional)

White or brown rice, or noodles, for serving (optional)

IN a small bowl, whisk together the soy sauce, brown sugar, oil, chili powder, red pepper flakes, and ginger. Pour the sauce into a large shallow dish or a large resealable bag. Add the steak and toss to coat well. Marinate for at least 3 hours or overnight.

REMOVE the steak from the marinade and add it to the air fryer basket along with the peppers and snow peas. Air fry at 380°F for 6 to 8 minutes, tossing halfway through, until the steak is no longer pink in the center.

TOSS with the sesame seeds, if desired, and serve warm over rice or noodles.

Tamale Pie

Tamale pie is a classic Tex-Mex comfort food. At its most basic, it's not much more than ground beef and a corn bread topping. But we've turned up the dial by mixing in enchilada sauce, chiles, olives, and cheese. Our families both love seeing this one on the menu for the week.

Serves 4

---

1 pound lean ground beef

1 (6-ounce) box Mexican-style corn bread mix (see Note)

1 (10-ounce) can red enchilada sauce

1 cup corn kernels (canned, frozen, or cooked fresh will work)

1 cup shredded mild or medium Cheddar

1 (4-ounce) can chopped green chiles

¼ cup sliced black olives

1 teaspoon chili powder

½ teaspoon garlic powder

IN a large skillet over medium heat, cook the beef while breaking it up with your spoon, until it is no longer pink, about 5 minutes. Set aside.

PREPARE the corn bread mix according to the directions on the box (aside from baking) and set aside.

IN an 8-inch round casserole or baking dish (glass or silicone), stir together the cooked beef with the enchilada sauce, corn, Cheddar, chiles, olives, chili powder, and garlic powder. Spread the corn bread mix over the top.

PLACE the casserole dish in the air fryer basket and air fry at 320°F for 15 to 17 minutes, until the corn bread is firm and golden brown. Serve warm.

NOTE: *We call for Mexican-style corn bread mix because it adds great flavor to the recipe, but any type of corn bread mix will work. Just keep in mind that a 6-ounce box will cover the pie perfectly. If you have a larger box, use ¾ cup of the prepared mix. Most mixes will call for just shy of 1 cup of whole milk and 1 egg.*

Whole Stuffed Chicken

It really doesn't get more impressive than a whole bird emerging golden, juicy, and piping hot from the oven. But we're not just talking about your Thanksgiving turkey, and we're definitely not just talking about special occasions. Nestling a whole chicken that's been slathered in seasonings into the air fryer is just about the easiest weeknight meal there is, especially when you stuff it with bell peppers and onion, which you can serve right alongside the perfectly cooked meat. Toss together a pot of rice or boil up some potatoes, and you have a very complete, very hearty meal.

Serves 4 to 6

1 (4-pound) chicken

1 green bell pepper, seeded and sliced

1 red bell pepper, seeded and sliced

½ medium yellow or white onion, sliced

1 lemon, quartered

½ teaspoon ground black pepper

½ teaspoon paprika

½ teaspoon garlic powder

Avocado or olive oil cooking spray (optional)

REMOVE any innards that may still be in the chicken, and pat the chicken dry with paper towels. Stuff the chicken with the bell peppers, onion, and lemon. Set aside.

IN a small bowl, stir together the black pepper, paprika, and garlic powder. Rub the mixture all over the skin of the chicken.

ADD 1 tablespoon of water to the tray below the air fryer basket. Lightly coat the basket with cooking spray or line it with a silicone baking mat. Place the chicken on top, breast side down, and air fry at 360°F for 20 minutes. Carefully flip the chicken over and air fry at 350°F for 40 to 45 minutes, until an instant-read thermometer inserted in the thickest part of the chicken reads 165°F.

TRANSFER the chicken to a cutting board, carve, and serve with the roasted peppers and onion.

Veggie
Mains

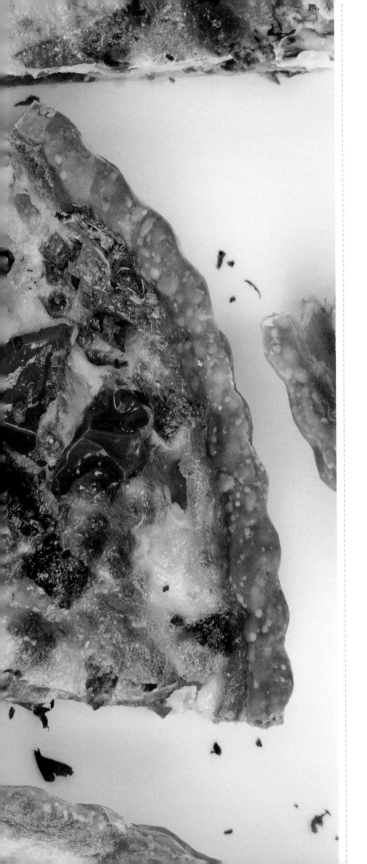

7

Don't get us wrong, we will always love our Whole Stuffed Chicken (page 136) and Filet and Mushrooms (page 102), but sometimes we want to lighten things up a little bit. And based on the feedback from our millions (!) of followers, we know that many of you feel that way, too. When we get this itch, we reach for recipes that deliver vegetable dishes that are just as flavorful and satisfying as our meat mains. But we get what a tall order that can be! That's why we wanted to dedicate an entire chapter to recipes that give vegetables the lead role. Here you'll find all your favorite produce players getting seasoned and sauced like the stars they're meant to be.

Cauliflower Steaks

This is one of our favorite "surprise" dishes—whenever we make it, someone is always shocked that cauliflower can be so savory and meaty. The trick is slathering these "steaks" in a seasoning blend first, then cooking them until golden and tender. Serve with your favorite steak house sides like Scalloped Red Potatoes (page 193) or Stuffed Baby Bella Mushrooms (page 188) for a fun vegetarian play on a classic steak meal.

Serves 3 to 4

1 large head of cauliflower

2 tablespoons extra-virgin olive oil

1 teaspoon lemon pepper

½ teaspoon garlic salt

¼ cup freshly grated Parmesan (optional)

REMOVE the leaves from the cauliflower and trim off the tough stem. Cut the cauliflower into 1-inch-thick slices (see Note). (We're usually able to get 3 to 4 slices per head of cauliflower.) Set aside.

IN a small bowl, combine the oil with the lemon pepper and garlic salt. Mix well. Brush the mixture over both sides of the cauliflower slices.

PLACE the steaks in the air fryer basket in a single layer. Top with the Parmesan (if using). Air fry at 380°F for 8 to 12 minutes, until the steaks are fork-tender.

NOTE: *Don't throw away any crumbling bits of cauliflower when you're done slicing the steaks! Toss them with the oil and seasoning mixture and air fry them until crispy.*

Cabbage Steaks

Whenever we're looking for a little extra oomph in the veggie department, this is the first dish that we reach for. When sliced into "steaks," slathered in seasoning, and air fried until tender in the center but crisp and caramelized around the edges, cabbage completely transforms into something hearty and savory. Serve this as a main alongside your favorite steak house sides or as a side dish with pretty much anything.

Serves 4

---

1 teaspoon ground black pepper

1 teaspoon garlic powder

½ teaspoon onion powder

1 medium head of green cabbage, cut into four 1-inch-wide slices

2 tablespoons extra-virgin olive oil

ADD ¼ cup water to the tray below the air fryer basket. Preheat the air fryer at 360°F for 3 minutes.

IN a small bowl, stir together the pepper, garlic powder, and onion powder.

BRUSH the cabbage steaks with oil on both sides, then sprinkle the seasonings over both sides of each steak. Arrange the steaks in a single layer in the air fryer and air fry at 360°F for 8 minutes. For crispier edges, cook for another 2 minutes.

STORE any leftovers in an airtight container in the refrigerator for up to 2 days. Reheat at 360°F for 2 minutes, or until warmed through.

Eggplant Parmesan

This is the ultimate one-and-done meal: It's substantial enough to be a main and comes with a vegetable baked right in. And the best part is that the air fryer takes care of both crisping up the eggplant and baking together the layers so that it tastes like a dish that took hours instead of minutes. Add the fact that it's not deep-fried like your favorite restaurant version, and you have a meal that you can feel really good about serving week after week.

Serves 4

---

1 medium eggplant, sliced into ¼-inch rounds

1 teaspoon sea salt

Avocado or olive oil cooking spray

1 large egg

½ cup panko bread crumbs

½ cup all-purpose flour

¼ cup freshly grated Parmesan

½ teaspoon ground black pepper

½ cup store-bought or homemade marinara sauce

½ cup shredded mozzarella

SPRINKLE the eggplant slices with ½ teaspoon of the salt (top and bottom) and place them in a large colander to drain for 30 minutes (see Note).

PREHEAT the air fryer to 370°F. Prepare the basket with the cooking spray and set aside.

IN a shallow bowl, whisk the egg. In another shallow bowl, combine the panko, flour, Parmesan, the remaining ½ teaspoon salt, and the pepper. Mix well.

PAT dry the eggplant slices with paper towels, then dip each slice in the egg, followed by the panko mixture. Arrange the coated eggplant on a baking sheet in a single layer as you work. When finished, spray the eggplant with the oil (about 1 teaspoon total).

TRANSFER the eggplant to the air fryer basket and lay the pieces in a single layer. (You may need to work in batches.) Air fry for 12 to 20 minutes, flipping the slices halfway through, until the eggplant is golden brown. Top each eggplant slice with 1 to 2 tablespoons of marinara and 2 teaspoons of mozzarella. Cook for an additional 2 minutes, until the cheese is bubbling and golden.

NOTE: *Don't skip salting and draining the eggplant! It's an extra step but one that ensures crispy eggplant.*

Ratatouille

This rustic French dish transforms roasted tomatoes, eggplants, zucchini, and squash into a hearty casserole scented with garlic and herbs. The key to getting the melt-in-your-mouth texture for the vegetables is to slice them very thin. We highly recommend using a mandoline for this dish, which is an inexpensive kitchen gadget that we guarantee you'll get good use out of—even if it's just to make this dish again and again!

Serves 4 to 6

---

1 (14.5-ounce) can crushed Roma-style tomatoes with roasted garlic

1 small to medium eggplant, thinly sliced

6 Roma tomatoes, thinly sliced

1 medium zucchini, thinly sliced

1 medium yellow squash, thinly sliced

2 tablespoons extra-virgin olive oil

1 teaspoon minced garlic

½ teaspoon sea salt

½ teaspoon dried basil

½ teaspoon dried thyme

¼ teaspoon ground black pepper

Rice or good, crusty bread, for serving (optional)

POUR the crushed tomatoes into the bottom of an 8-inch round casserole or baking dish (glass or silicone). Top with a layer of eggplant slices arranged in a circular pattern with each slice overlapping. (You won't use all of the eggplant in the first layer.) Layer the tomato slices in the same way, followed by zucchini slices and squash slices. Continue layering all of the vegetables in this way (see Note) until no more slices are left or you've run out of room in your baking dish.

IN a small bowl, stir together the oil, garlic, salt, basil, thyme, and pepper. Drizzle the mixture over the top of the vegetables.

CAREFULLY place the dish in the air fryer basket and air fry at 350°F for 15 to 18 minutes, until the vegetables are tender. Serve with rice or bread, if desired.

NOTE: *Here we call for you to make individual layers of each vegetable, but for an even more colorful presentation, alternate the vegetables in a circular pattern, adding layers until the dish is filled. Take care not to overfill the dish or pack the vegetables too tightly, or they won't cook properly.*

Sesame-Garlic Tofu and Vegetables

We challenge anyone who thinks tofu isn't flavorful or satisfying enough for dinner to try this recipe. Not only does the tofu get delectably crispy, it also gets a savory glaze of soy sauce, garlic, and sesame oil. Combined with a well-seasoned vegetable medley, it's the kind of dish that you feel just as good serving as you do eating. We highly recommend cooking up a pot of rice or noodles to make this meal feel even more satisfying—and for sopping up all that saucy goodness.

Serves 4

FOR THE SESAME GARLIC TOFU

16 ounces extra-firm tofu

¼ cup soy sauce or liquid aminos

1 tablespoon sesame oil

2 teaspoons minced garlic

1 teaspoon sesame seeds

2 tablespoons cornstarch

FOR THE VEGETABLES

1 red bell pepper, seeded and sliced

1 cup broccoli florets

1 cup fresh snow peas

10 cherry or grape tomatoes, halved

1 tablespoon sesame or extra-virgin olive oil

½ teaspoon sea salt

½ teaspoon garlic powder

¼ teaspoon ground black pepper

FOR SERVING

Rice or noodles, for serving (optional)

MAKE the sesame garlic tofu: Drain the tofu and wrap it in paper towels. Set a weight (such as a pan) on top to press the tofu for 30 minutes. Cut the tofu into 1-inch cubes and place them in a large bowl. Add the soy sauce, sesame oil, garlic, and sesame seeds and gently toss to coat the tofu. Let the tofu marinate for 15 to 30 minutes.

SPRINKLE the cornstarch over the tofu and toss to coat. Add the tofu to the air fryer basket and air fry at 380°F for 10 minutes.

WHILE the tofu is cooking, make the vegetables: In a large bowl, combine the bell pepper, broccoli, snow peas, and tomatoes with the olive oil, salt, garlic powder, and black pepper. Mix well to coat the vegetables.

ONCE the tofu has cooked for 10 minutes, give it a toss in the air fryer basket, then add the vegetables and toss together. Air fry at 380°F for another 10 minutes, until the tofu is crispy and the vegetables are tender.

SERVE with rice or noodles, if desired.

Stuffed Eggplant

Eggplant is one of our favorite vegetables for a vegetarian main because it's naturally "meaty" in flavor and texture. We especially love to serve entire halves, which get stuffed with a cheesy, saucy filling. It's a dish that is just as delicious and satisfying as it looks—which makes it the perfect meal for any veggie skeptics out there.

Serves 2

---

1 large eggplant

1 tablespoon extra-virgin olive oil

1 cup shredded or torn mozzarella

¼ cup shredded or grated Parmesan

¾ cup marinara sauce

¼ cup Italian-seasoned bread crumbs

1 tablespoon dried parsley flakes

½ teaspoon sea salt

½ teaspoon garlic powder

¼ teaspoon ground black pepper

SLICE off the stem end of the eggplant and discard, then slice the eggplant in half lengthwise. Use a spoon to gently scoop out the center of the eggplant, leaving about a ½-inch border around the edges. Reserve the scooped eggplant and set aside. Brush both cut sides of the eggplant with the oil.

PLACE the eggplant halves cut side up in the air fryer basket and air fry at 400°F for 10 to 15 minutes, flipping the eggplant over halfway through cooking. You want the eggplant to be tender.

WHILE the eggplant cooks, place the reserved eggplant in a small pot and add enough water just to cover. Bring to a boil, reduce to a simmer, and cook until the eggplant is tender, 3 to 5 minutes. Strain the eggplant and mash it with a fork or potato masher until it's not quite completely smooth. Allow it to cool slightly while you assemble the filling.

IN a medium bowl, toss together the mozzarella and Parmesan. Add the marinara, bread crumbs, parsley, salt, garlic powder, and pepper and stir to combine. Once the eggplant has cooled, stir it into the filling.

WHEN the eggplant halves are done cooking, flip them so they're once again cut side up and fill each half with the filling. Air fry again for 3 to 5 minutes, until the cheese has melted.

Spaghetti Squash Marinara

Spaghetti squash is the secret weapon of the produce aisle. The inside of the squash both looks and feels just like strands of spaghetti and, when cooked, has a mild taste. That means that you can do it up just like the ideal bowl of pasta—smothered in marinara sauce and Parmesan. Because you already have your veg cooked right in, you could serve this and call it a meal, or pair it with a side of good, crusty bread to feel like you've gone to your favorite Italian restaurant.

Serves 2

1 medium spaghetti squash (it should be able to fit into the air fryer basket)

1 tablespoon extra-virgin olive oil

½ teaspoon sea salt

½ teaspoon ground black pepper

½ cup prepared or store-bought marinara sauce

¼ cup shredded or grated Parmesan

SLICE the spaghetti squash in half lengthwise. Use a spoon to scoop out the seeds and discard.

RUB the inside of the squash with the oil and season with the salt and pepper. Place the squash flesh side up in the air fryer and air fry at 370°F for 25 to 30 minutes, until the squash is fork-tender. Allow the squash to cool slightly before removing it from the air fryer.

USE a fork to gently scrape and "lift" the flesh to loosen and separate the strands. Top each slice with ¼ cup of the marinara and 2 tablespoons of the Parmesan and serve.

Tofu and Veggie Fajitas

One of the most popular nights in our houses is steak and veggie fajita night, so we wanted to come up with a meat-free version that was just as flavorful. Tofu has a great meaty texture, especially after you've pressed out most of the liquid, and has a mild flavor that's great for showing off all those classic fajita seasonings. We love serving these with all the toppings, then enjoying any leftovers over rice or tossed with greens for a fajita salad.

Serves 4

Avocado or olive oil cooking spray, or extra-virgin olive oil

16 ounces extra-firm tofu

1 tablespoon chili powder

1 teaspoon ground cumin

1 teaspoon garlic powder

1 teaspoon ground coriander

1 teaspoon sea salt

1 red bell pepper, seeded and sliced

1 green bell pepper, seeded and sliced

1 yellow bell pepper, seeded and sliced

1 medium yellow or white onion, sliced

12 (6-inch) corn or flour tortillas

Your favorite fajita toppings, for serving (see Note)

LIGHTLY coat the air fryer basket with the cooking spray or oil and set aside. Drain the tofu and wrap it in paper towels. Place a weight (such as a small pan) on top to press the tofu for 30 minutes.

IN a medium bowl, mix together the chili powder, cumin, garlic powder, coriander, and salt. Set aside.

SLICE the tofu into roughly ½ × 2-inch strips. Add the tofu, peppers, and onion to the seasoning mixture and toss to coat. Transfer the mixture to the air fryer basket.

AIR fry at 380°F for 13 to 15 minutes, tossing every few minutes to ensure even cooking. You want the peppers to be tender and the tofu to be warmed through.

SERVE the tofu and veggies with the tortillas and your favorite fajita toppings. Store any leftovers in an airtight container in the refrigerator for up to 3 days.

NOTE: *If you're in a hurry or don't have some of these spices on hand, you can substitute the fajita seasoning with 4 tablespoons of taco or Mexican seasoning. Our favorite toppings to include with this dish are sliced avocado, sour cream, shredded cheese, lime juice, and diced jalapeños.*

Vegetable Pot Pie

A creamy, vegetable-studded pot pie with a flaky crust is pretty much the ideal comfort food meal. And yet once you assemble all the components, it's a little more work than most people want to do for a weeknight dinner (or any meal, really). That's why we made it our goal to come up with a version that delivers that same rich, velvety gravy and buttery crust but requires a fraction of the effort and the time. The added bonus is that even though this version doesn't call for any meat, it is still sumptuous and satisfying.

Serves 6

⅓ cup (5 tablespoons) unsalted butter

½ medium yellow onion, sliced (about ½ cup)

1 teaspoon minced garlic

½ cup all-purpose flour, plus more for dusting

1¼ cups vegetable broth

1 cup whole milk

1 teaspoon sea salt

½ teaspoon ground black pepper

1 cup sliced portobello or white mushrooms

1 cup broccoli florets cut into bite-sized pieces

1 cup sliced carrots (about 2 large carrots)

½ cup cauliflower florets cut into bite-sized pieces

1 package store-bought pie dough

IN a large saucepan over medium heat, combine the butter, onion, and garlic and cook until the onion softens, about 3 minutes. Remove the pan from the heat.

WHISK in the flour, followed by the broth, milk, salt, and pepper. Return the pan to medium heat and cook, continuing to stir, until the sauce thickens and slowly begins to bubble, about 5 minutes. Remove the pan from the heat. Stir in the vegetables (see Note) until well combined, then transfer the mixture to an 8-inch round casserole or baking dish (glass or silicone).

LIGHTLY flour a work surface. Use a rolling pin to roll out the pie crust to ⅛-inch thickness. Cover the entire top of the casserole dish with the crust, then trim the edges. Use a knife to cut four to six 1-inch vents in the top or pierce all over with a fork.

PLACE the casserole dish in the air fryer basket and air fry at 350°F for 13 to 15 minutes, until the crust is golden brown and crisp.

NOTE: *A time-saving shortcut is to use a large bag of frozen California-style mixed vegetables instead of the fresh chopped vegetables. You'll need 3 to 4 cups total.*

Mushroom and Spinach Quiche

We know a quiche might sound kinda fussy, but when you see how easy it is to whip together a veggie-packed filling and pour it into a store-bought pie crust, you'll realize what a great recipe this is to have in your easy-meal arsenal. Yet with one bite of this cheesy, flaky-crust heaven, you'd never guess it was that simple to pull together. Feel free to mix and match different vegetable mix-ins or even different cheeses.

Serves 4

All-purpose flour, for dusting

1 package store-bought pie dough

4 large eggs

¼ cup heavy cream or whole milk

½ cup shredded mild Cheddar

¼ cup chopped baby portobello mushrooms

¼ cup chopped or torn fresh spinach leaves

¼ cup crumbled feta

¼ cup chopped yellow onion

6 cherry or grape tomatoes, halved or quartered

½ teaspoon sea salt

¼ teaspoon ground black pepper

LIGHTLY dust a work surface with the flour. Use a rolling pin to roll out the crust to ⅛-inch thickness and transfer it to an 8-inch tart pan or pie plate. Trim the edges and press the crust firmly into the sides of the pan. Use a fork to dot the bottom of the crust with holes and smooth out any pockets of air.

TRANSFER the pan to the air fryer basket and air fry at 350°F for 7 to 9 minutes, until the crust is light golden brown. Set aside to cool.

MEANWHILE, make the filling. In a medium bowl, whisk together the eggs and cream until well combined. Stir in the Cheddar, mushrooms, spinach, feta, onion, tomatoes, salt, and pepper. Pour the filling into the cooled crust.

AIR fry at 350°F for 5 minutes. Open the air fryer and gently stir the filling to keep the solids from settling at the bottom. Air fry for another 8 to 12 minutes, until the filling has fluffed slightly and is firm to the touch. Serve warm, at room temperature, or chilled.

Vegetables au Gratin

It almost seems like cheating, but the best way to transform vegetables into a decadent main dish is to add cream, cheese, butter, and bread crumbs. The medley of vegetables gets perfectly tender in the air fryer while the buttery bread crumb topping turns crisp and golden. These delicious layers of texture and flavor make this dish a crowd-pleaser—for kids and adults—every single time!

Serves 4

Avocado or olive oil cooking spray, or extra-virgin olive oil

1 (12-ounce) bag frozen California-style vegetables (see Note)

2 cups shredded mild or medium Cheddar

½ cup shredded or grated Parmesan

½ cup finely chopped white or yellow onion

1 teaspoon minced garlic

½ teaspoon sea salt

¼ teaspoon ground black pepper

1 cup heavy cream

½ cup panko bread crumbs

2 tablespoons unsalted butter, melted

LIGHTLY coat an 8-inch round casserole or baking dish (glass or silicone) with the cooking spray or oil and set aside.

IN a large bowl, combine the vegetables, Cheddar, Parmesan, onion, garlic, salt, and pepper. Mix well. Transfer the mixture to the prepared casserole dish, then pour the cream over the top.

PLACE the casserole dish in the air fryer basket and air fry at 350°F for 15 to 18 minutes, stirring about halfway through, until the cheese has melted and the vegetables have softened.

MEANWHILE, in a small bowl, stir together the panko and butter. When the vegetables are done cooking, spread the panko mixture evenly over the top. Air fry for an additional 5 to 6 minutes, until the topping is golden brown.

NOTE: *You could substitute any chopped fresh vegetables—or another variety of frozen vegetables—for the California-style vegetables. You'll just need about 2 cups of vegetables total. We like to rinse our frozen vegetables under cold water for a minute before using them to break up any big chunks.*

Seafood Mains

8

For many people, making seafood dishes at home can feel overwhelming. Or maybe you've tried and it hasn't gone so well. Maybe your fish stuck to your (supposedly nonstick) pan, or it dried out on you, or it just didn't taste like it did the one time you had it in the restaurant. No matter what you may have been up against, we've got the solutions on all counts. The beauty of these recipes is that they take all of the guesswork out of how to not only properly cook seafood but also prepare it in a way that rivals the fanciest dining establishment. Whether it's crispy Coconut Shrimp (page 158) you're in the mood for, simple Scallops and Tomatoes with Creamy Pesto Sauce (page 175), or sumptuous Lobster Tails (page 164), this chapter will have everyone wanting to kiss the chef.

Coconut Shrimp

Something magical happens when you toss shrimp with paprika-spiked coconut flakes and cook them until golden and crisp. It's a little bit meaty, a little bit sweet, a little bit smoky, and a whole lot of delicious. To really play up the coconut flavor, we use coconut flour here instead of bread crumbs (which also happens to make this low-carb and keto-friendly, if that's something you're mindful of).

Serves 4

Avocado or olive oil cooking spray (optional)

½ cup coconut flour (see Note)

1 tablespoon ground black pepper

1 teaspoon smoked paprika

3 large eggs, beaten

1¾ cups unsweetened coconut flakes

25 large (21/25) shrimp, peeled and deveined

Cocktail sauce, remoulade, or French dressing, for serving (optional)

PREHEAT the air fryer to 390°F. Lightly spray the air fryer basket with cooking spray or line with air fryer parchment paper. Set aside.

IN a medium bowl, combine the coconut flour, pepper, and paprika. Mix well. Add the beaten eggs to a second medium bowl and the coconut flakes to a third.

DIP the shrimp into the coconut flour mixture to coat well, then the eggs, and finally into the coconut flakes. Set the coated shrimp on a wire rack and continue with the remaining shrimp.

ARRANGE the coated shrimp in a single layer in the air fryer basket, working in batches if necessary, and cook for 10 to 12 minutes, flipping halfway through, until the shrimp are golden and crisp. Serve immediately with any desired dipping sauces.

NOTE: *Although it doesn't have the same subtle coconutty flavor as coconut flour, using bread crumbs instead will give you an even crispier texture. To make the swap, use ¼ cup bread crumbs plus ¼ cup panko bread crumbs.*

Bacon-Wrapped Shrimp

It doesn't get simpler—or more delicious—than wrapping shrimp in bacon and cooking it until it's perfectly juicy on the inside and delectably crispy on the outside. Plus, thanks to a spice and brown sugar rub, this dish is both sweet and smoky with a touch of heat. Whether you're putting these out for dinner or as an appetizer, you can serve them on their own or with remoulade sauce for dipping.

Serves 4

Avocado or olive oil cooking spray (optional)

1 teaspoon ground black pepper

½ teaspoon smoked paprika

½ teaspoon packed brown sugar

1 pound large (21/25) shrimp, peeled and deveined (see Note)

8 slices thin-cut bacon, cut into thirds

Prepared or store-bought remoulade sauce, for serving (optional)

LIGHTLY spray the air fryer basket with cooking spray or line with air fryer parchment paper. Set aside.

IN a small bowl, combine the pepper, paprika, and brown sugar. Mix well.

LAY the shrimp on a baking sheet and sprinkle them evenly with seasonings. Wrap each shrimp with a piece of the bacon. Arrange the bacon-wrapped shrimp in a single layer in the air fryer basket.

COOK at 390°F for 9 to 10 minutes, until the bacon is crisp and the shrimp is no longer translucent. There is no need to pause and flip the shrimp. Serve hot with dipping sauce, if desired.

BEST served immediately. Leftovers can be stored in an airtight container in the refrigerator for up to 4 days. Reheat in the air fryer on 300°F for 2 to 3 minutes on each side.

NOTE: *Keep the tails on the shrimp or take them off, depending on your preference.*

Crab Legs

There's a reason why this dish is a fan favorite—it takes minutes to come together, and yet it is so impressive and indulgent. You could serve this on its own with a simple side as dinner, offer it to guests as a fun appetizer, or make it part of a festive seafood spread with Lobster Tails (page 164) or Bacon-Wrapped Shrimp (page 161)—or both!

Serves 1 to 2

1 pound snow crab legs

1 tablespoon extra-virgin olive oil

1 teaspoon Old Bay seasoning

2 tablespoons unsalted butter, melted (optional)

LIGHTLY rinse the crab legs under cold water to remove any sand or dirt.

IN a medium bowl, toss the crab legs with the oil and Old Bay seasoning to coat.

COOK at 370°F for 5 to 7 minutes, until the shells are hot to the touch. Serve with the melted butter for dipping, if desired.

Tuna and Noodles

There was a time when an old-school version of this dish would be on our respective dinner tables at least once a week. It made sense—it was inexpensive to make, took barely any time to prepare, but even the pickiest of eaters wouldn't have turned down this creamy, cheesy goodness. Far be it from us to dramatically change such a beloved standby dish, so we've just given it a little freshening up with peas and mushrooms.

Serves 6

3 cups (6 ounces) uncooked medium egg noodles

1 (10.5-ounce) can condensed cream of mushroom soup

2 (5-ounce) cans tuna in water, drained

1 cup frozen green peas

½ cup sliced portobello or white mushrooms

¼ cup heavy cream

1 teaspoon garlic powder

½ teaspoon sea salt

¼ teaspoon ground black pepper

½ cup Italian-seasoned bread crumbs

¼ cup grated Parmesan or mild or medium Cheddar

IN a medium saucepan over high heat, bring 3 cups water to a boil. Add the noodles and cook, covered, until the noodles are tender, 6 to 8 minutes. Drain.

ADD the noodles to a large bowl with the soup, tuna, peas, mushrooms, cream, garlic powder, salt, and pepper. Toss to combine.

TRANSFER the mixture to an 8-inch round casserole or baking dish (glass or silicone). Air fry at 350°F for 5 minutes. Sprinkle the bread crumbs over the top of the noodles, then continue cooking for another 5 minutes.

TOP with the Parmesan while still hot and serve warm.

Lobster Tails

Since launching our Air Frying Foodie Facebook group, we've loved seeing the hundreds—if not thousands—of rave reviews for this recipe. Not only does it demystify how to make such a "fancy" delicacy in your own home, but it also makes for such a delicious meal with just a few simple seasonings. When it comes to lobster, we find that less is more—just butter, garlic, lemon, and a hint of Old Bay.

Serves 2

---

2 (6- to 8-ounce) lobster tails

2 tablespoons unsalted butter, melted, plus more for brushing

2 garlic cloves, minced or pressed

1 teaspoon lemon juice

½ teaspoon sea salt

½ teaspoon ground black pepper

¼ teaspoon Old Bay seasoning

LINE the air fryer basket with air fryer parchment paper and set aside.

CUT the top of each lobster's shell so that you can pull the meat up to rest on the shell. Carefully split the meat down the center without cutting all the way through using a knife. Place the lobster tails in the air fryer basket and set aside.

IN a small bowl, stir together the butter, garlic, lemon juice, salt, pepper, and Old Bay. Brush the mixture over the top of each lobster tail, coating the meat well.

AIR fry at 380°F for 3 minutes. Brush the tails with more butter, then continue cooking for another 3 to 5 minutes, until the meat is white and an instant-read thermometer inserted in the center of the tail reads 135° to 140°F.

Salmon and Rice Bake

Not only is this dish delicious and hearty and everything else you'd want in an easy weeknight meal, but it also calls for items that are almost always in your fridge and pantry (especially if you keep tins of salmon around, which we recommend you do!). It's the perfect example of a recipe that is greater than the sum of its humble parts.

Serves 4

---

1 large egg

½ cup whole milk

1 cup white rice, cooked according to the package instructions

1 (14.75-ounce) can pink salmon, drained and flaked with a fork

½ cup shredded or grated Parmesan

1 tablespoon dried parsley flakes

1 teaspoon garlic powder

1 teaspoon sea salt

½ cup panko bread crumbs

¼ cup (4 tablespoons) unsalted butter, melted

IN a medium bowl, whisk together the egg and milk. Add the cooked rice, salmon, Parmesan, parsley, garlic powder, and salt. Stir until well combined, then transfer the mixture to an 8-inch round casserole or baking dish (glass or silicone). Set aside.

IN a small bowl, stir together the panko and butter. Spoon the mixture over the top of the salmon and rice mixture.

PLACE the dish in the air fryer basket. Air fry at 350°F for 6 to 8 minutes, until the panko is golden brown and crispy. Serve warm.

Fish Tacos

There is no quicker way to feel like you're on a beach vacation than whipping up a batch of fish tacos. Luckily, that doesn't have to take more than 15 minutes, thanks to this tried-and-true recipe. All it entails is dressing up whitefish with a smoky spice mix, then loading up a tortilla with your favorite toppings and our three-ingredient spicy lime crema. Let's just say that your Taco Tuesday is in for a major upgrade!

Makes 6 tacos (serves 3)

FOR THE FISH

1 teaspoon garlic powder

1 teaspoon onion powder

1 teaspoon paprika

1 teaspoon chili powder

½ teaspoon kosher salt

2 (6-ounce) whitefish fillets, such as cod, tilapia, catfish, or mahi-mahi

1 tablespoon extra-virgin olive oil

FOR THE SPICY LIME CREMA

½ cup sour cream

¼ cup hot sauce

1 teaspoon fresh lime juice

FOR ASSEMBLY

6 small (5.5- to 6-inch) flour or corn tortillas

1 cup shredded purple cabbage, for serving (optional)

1 medium avocado, sliced, for serving (optional)

½ medium red onion, diced, for serving (optional)

1 cup crumbled cotija, for serving (optional)

Fresh cilantro, for serving (optional)

MAKE the fish: In a small bowl, mix together the garlic powder, onion powder, paprika, chili powder, and salt. Lightly brush both sides of the fish fillets with the oil, and then coat with the seasoning mix. Place the fillets in a single layer in the air fryer basket and air fry at 350°F for 6 to 7 minutes, until an instant-read thermometer inserted in the center reads 145°F.

WHILE the fish cooks, make the spicy lime crema: In a small bowl, stir together the sour cream, hot sauce, and lime juice. Set aside.

ASSEMBLE the tacos: Use your fingers or two forks to shred the cooked fish into bite-sized flakes. Fill the tortillas with the fish, add any desired toppings, and drizzle with the crema. Serve immediately.

Creole Blackened Haddock

A batch of fish in the air fryer is one of the easiest, quickest meals you can make, and it's major bonus points that it also happens to feel healthy and light. But we get that regularly cooking fish can also get a little . . . boring. So we came up with this Creole rub with spices like thyme, oregano, cayenne, and red pepper flakes to transform mild, flaky halibut into the kind of main you look forward to week after week. Serve this over pasta, with a veggie side or two, or wrap the fish in tortillas for (nearly) instant fish tacos.

Serves 2

½ teaspoon cayenne pepper

½ teaspoon crushed red pepper flakes

½ teaspoon ground black pepper

½ teaspoon onion powder

½ teaspoon ground white pepper

½ teaspoon dried thyme

½ teaspoon dried oregano

2 (5-ounce) haddock fillets

1 tablespoon extra-virgin olive oil

1 tablespoon fresh lemon juice

IN a small bowl, mix together the cayenne, red pepper flakes, black pepper, onion powder, white pepper, thyme, and oregano. Set aside.

BRUSH both sides of each fillet with the oil, then sprinkle with the seasoning mixture.

PLACE the fillets in a single layer in the air fryer basket and air fry at 400°F for 8 to 10 minutes, until the fish flakes with a fork. Top with the lemon juice before serving.

Cajun Mahi-Mahi with Vegetables

Not only will this recipe ensure that you (yes, you!) can get perfectly tender, flaky, flavorful fish every time you cook it, it's also one of those great easy-to-make, easy-to-serve mains that delivers a protein *and* veggies in one go. Though the big, bold Cajun rub makes this dish taste anything but simple!

Serves 2

FOR THE MAHI-MAHI
½ teaspoon cayenne pepper
½ teaspoon crushed red pepper flakes
½ teaspoon ground black pepper
2 (6- to 8-ounce) mahi-mahi fillets
1 tablespoon extra-virgin olive oil
1 tablespoon fresh lemon juice, for serving

FOR THE ROASTED VEGETABLES
1 medium red bell pepper, seeded and sliced
1 medium yellow bell pepper, seeded and sliced
1 small zucchini, sliced
8 cherry tomatoes, halved
1 tablespoon extra-virgin olive oil
½ teaspoon cayenne pepper
½ teaspoon crushed red pepper flakes
¼ teaspoon ground black pepper

MAKE the mahi-mahi: In a small bowl, combine the cayenne, red pepper flakes, and black pepper.

BRUSH both sides of each fillet with the oil and sprinkle evenly with the seasoning mixture. Place the fillets in a single layer on one side of the air fryer basket and set aside.

MAKE the roasted vegetables: In a large bowl, combine the bell peppers, zucchini, and tomatoes with the oil, cayenne, red pepper flakes, and black pepper. Toss to coat the vegetables well.

ADD the vegetables to the other side of the air fryer basket and air fry at 400°F for 8 to 10 minutes, until the vegetables are tender and the fish flakes easily with a fork. Sprinkle everything with lemon juice and serve.

Scallops and Tomatoes with Creamy Pesto Sauce

Scallops are an amazing seafood to incorporate into your dinner rotation. They're quick cooking, taste substantial and meaty, and get along well with lots of other flavors. Here we're combining them with garlicky roasted tomatoes and a decadent, cheesy pesto sauce. Tossed with pasta, it's the kind of dish that will have people begging to come back again for dinner.

Serves 4

FOR THE SCALLOPS AND TOMATOES

8 to 10 large (30/40) sea scallops

12 cherry or grape tomatoes, quartered or halved

1 tablespoon prepared or store-bought basil pesto

1 teaspoon minced garlic

½ teaspoon sea salt

Pinch of ground black pepper

8 ounces spaghetti or fettuccine, cooked according to the package instructions

FOR THE CREAMY PESTO SAUCE

1 tablespoon prepared or store-bought basil pesto

1 teaspoon minced garlic

1½ cups heavy cream

1 tablespoon all-purpose flour

½ teaspoon sea salt

2 tablespoons shredded or grated Parmesan

MAKE the scallops and tomatoes: Pat the scallops dry with a paper towel. In a medium bowl, combine the scallops, tomatoes, pesto, garlic, salt, and pepper. Mix until the scallops and tomatoes are evenly coated.

PLACE the mixture in the air fryer basket and air fry at 400°F for 9 to 11 minutes, until the scallops are slightly firm and golden brown.

MEANWHILE, make the creamy pesto sauce: In a small saucepan over medium heat, whisk together the pesto and garlic. Heat for 1 minute to let the flavors meld, then whisk in the cream, flour, and salt. Whisk until the sauce begins to simmer and thicken, 3 to 5 minutes. Remove the pan from the heat and whisk in the Parmesan until melted.

IN a serving bowl, top the pasta with the creamy pesto sauce, tomatoes, and scallops. Serve hot.

Spicy Garlic Shrimp

Don't be deceived by the small number of ingredients here—this dish brings some seriously deep, complex flavor. By cooking the shrimp in a garlicky, spicy butter, you end up with a pan sauce flavored with all the cooking juices that begs to be spooned over rice or pasta (or enjoyed all on its own, as we often do). The recipe comes together in 10 minutes, but your family or guests would never guess it.

Serves 4

1 pound medium or large shrimp, peeled and deveined

¼ cup (4 tablespoons) unsalted butter, melted

1 teaspoon minced garlic

1 teaspoon chili powder

1 teaspoon crushed red pepper flakes

White or brown rice, or pasta, for serving (optional)

RINSE the shrimp under cold water and pat dry with a paper towel. Set aside.

IN a large bowl, stir together the butter, garlic, chili powder, and red pepper flakes. Add the shrimp and toss to coat well.

POUR the shrimp and any butter mixture into the air fryer basket. Arrange the shrimp so they aren't overlapping. Air fry at 370°F for 6 to 8 minutes, tossing halfway through, until the shrimp are opaque and no longer translucent.

SERVE over rice or pasta, if desired.

Sides

9

Sides may not be the main event for most meals, but when they're made well with loads of flavor, they have a way of stealing the show. Or at the very least making a meal feel more thoughtful and satisfying. But we would never want a side dish to take up any more of your precious time than is necessary, so we've come up with a solid roster of recipes that will add a lot to your spread without adding a lot of time or effort to your meal prep. Feel free to mix and match these dishes with meat, seafood, or veg mains for your meals at home, or use them as inspiration the next time you need to bring a dish for a potluck or holiday.

Sweet Potato Casserole

There is no better dish for the holidays than this casserole, and we've made it super easy for you to whip it up alongside any of the other staples that fill your family's table. But don't forget about this recipe once January rolls around! It would be just as at home next to your favorite mains at dinnertime, no matter the season (just maybe sans marshmallow fluff).

Serves 4

Avocado or olive oil cooking spray

¾ cup finely chopped pecans (optional)

1 (29-ounce) can sweet potatoes, drained

1¼ cups granulated sugar

2 tablespoons unsalted butter, softened

1 large egg

1 tablespoon heavy cream

½ teaspoon vanilla extract

¼ teaspoon sea salt

¼ teaspoon ground cinnamon

1 (7.5-ounce) jar of marshmallow fluff (optional; see Note)

PREHEAT the air fryer to 350°F. Lightly grease an 8-inch round casserole or baking dish (glass or silicone) with cooking spray and set aside.

IN a food processor, pulse the pecans (if using) just until they are fine enough to sprinkle. You could also do this in a plastic zip-top bag and pound them with a meat mallet, rolling pin, or small pan. Set aside.

IN a medium bowl, combine the sweet potatoes with the sugar, butter, egg, cream, vanilla, salt, and cinnamon. Mix thoroughly for 1 minute until the ingredients are evenly incorporated.

TRANSFER the sweet potato mixture to the prepared baking dish. Cover with the pecans and/or marshmallow fluff (if using). Place the dish in the air fryer basket and air fry for 10 to 12 minutes, until the nuts are lightly browned and the marshmallow fluff is golden. Serve warm.

NOTE: *Feel free to make this with pecans, marshmallows, or both. However, unlike your usual sweet potato casserole recipe that calls for mini marshmallows, we suggest using marshmallow fluff instead. Marshmallows have a habit of flying around while air frying because of the fan. Though you could also push them into the casserole to secure them.*

Corn Casserole

Whether you need a feel-good side for a weeknight, a dish to bring to a barbecue or potluck, or a dish worthy of your holiday table, this casserole is all of the above. It's creamy, buttery, slightly sweet, and comes together in no time.

Serves 4

---

1 (15.25-ounce) can corn kernels, drained

1 (14.75-ounce) can creamed corn

⅔ cup sour cream

¼ cup (4 tablespoons) unsalted butter, melted

½ teaspoon sea salt

¼ teaspoon ground black pepper

1 (8.5-ounce) box Jiffy corn muffin mix

1 large egg

⅓ cup whole milk

IN a medium bowl, combine the corn kernels, creamed corn, sour cream, butter, salt, and pepper. Mix well. Transfer the mixture to an 8-inch round casserole or baking dish (glass or silicone).

IN another medium bowl, prepare the muffin mix according to the package instructions, with the egg and milk. Pour the batter evenly over the corn mixture and spread to cover the entire top of the casserole.

PLACE the casserole dish in the air fryer basket and air fry at 320°F for 15 to 17 minutes, until the casserole is golden.

Jalapeño Poppers

This cheesy, bacony snack is ten times better than anything you can buy in the freezer aisle, and yet these poppers take just as little time to cook. Air frying them not only helps make prep more efficient, it also gets the bacon to the exact crispness that you want. Unsurprisingly, these are a go-to favorite for both of our families and for many of our followers.

Serves 4

6 medium jalapeños

4 ounces plain cream cheese

12 slices of bacon (see Note)

SLICE the jalapeños in half lengthwise. Remove all the seeds and rinse the jalapeños. Blot dry with paper towels and set aside.

CUT the cream cheese into 12 strips (see Note). Place a strip inside each jalapeño half. Wrap a piece of bacon around each half, securing it with a toothpick.

ARRANGE the poppers in a single layer in the air fryer basket, working in batches if necessary. Air fry at 370°F for 10 to 12 minutes, until the bacon is browned and crispy. Allow the poppers to cool—just for a minute so the center won't be so molten hot!—before enjoying them.

NOTE: *If you can only find smaller jalapeños, wrap the poppers with just half a slice of bacon. Also, it will be easier to slice the cream cheese if it is chilled.*

Asparagus and Tofu Salad with Italian Vinaigrette

We can't decide what's most surprising about this dish—the fact that something so light and fresh is made possible by an air fryer, how filling and flavorful a salad can be, or how well roasted asparagus and crispy sesame-soy tofu go together. When tossed with tomatoes, olives, mozzarella, and tangy vinaigrette, it's perfect as part of a weeknight meal or on its own as part of a potluck or barbecue spread.

Serves 4

FOR THE TOFU AND ASPARAGUS

16 ounces extra-firm tofu

1 tablespoon sesame oil

2 tablespoons cornstarch

¼ cup soy sauce

1 large bunch of asparagus (about 1 pound)

1 tablespoon extra-virgin olive oil

½ teaspoon sea salt

¼ teaspoon ground black pepper

FOR THE SALAD

10 cherry or grape tomatoes, halved

10 kalamata olives, pitted and halved

½ cup mozzarella pearls, or 6 to 8 small slices

2 tablespoons Italian dressing

1 tablespoon slivered almonds

MAKE the tofu and asparagus: Drain the tofu and wrap it in paper towels. Place a weight (such as a small pan) on top to press the tofu for 30 minutes. Cut the tofu into 1-inch cubes and place them in a large bowl. Toss to coat with the sesame oil. Add the cornstarch and once again toss to coat. Toss once more with the soy sauce and let the tofu marinate for 15 to 30 minutes.

TRIM the fibrous ends of the asparagus and discard. A helpful trick is to gently bend the asparagus—it will snap in the right spot. We usually keep the asparagus whole for this recipe, but you could cut the spears into bite-sized pieces. Add the asparagus to a large bowl with the olive oil, salt, and pepper and toss to coat well.

(recipe continues)

FILL a large bowl with ice water and set aside. Arrange the asparagus on one side of the air fryer basket and the tofu on the other. Air fry at 380°F for 8 to 10 minutes, tossing the asparagus halfway through. When the asparagus is tender, transfer it to the ice bath to cool. Strain and set aside.

TOSS the tofu in the air fryer basket and cook for an additional 15 to 18 minutes, until crispy. Allow to cool slightly before assembling the salad.

ASSEMBLE the salad: In a large bowl, combine the tofu and asparagus with the tomatoes, olives, mozzarella, and dressing. Toss to combine. Sprinkle with the almonds and serve.

Parmesan Brussels Sprouts

One of the biggest reasons why this recipe has become a fan favorite many, many, many times over is because people can't believe that they can make perfectly crispy brussels sprouts in their own kitchen—not to mention with a fraction of the oil and salt they would be prepared with in a restaurant. To take these to the next level, we've added garlic and Parmesan, which make these a standout side dish or even an appetizer.

Serves 2 to 4

---

1 pound of brussels sprouts	½ teaspoon kosher or sea salt
1 tablespoon extra-virgin olive oil	Pinch of ground black pepper
2 garlic cloves, pressed or minced	½ cup shredded or grated Parmesan

---

PREHEAT the air fryer to 400°F.

CUT the brussels sprouts in half and rinse them under running water. Pat dry with a kitchen towel or paper towels.

PLACE the brussels sprouts in a large bowl. Drizzle over the oil and add the garlic. Give everything a toss until the sprouts are well coated. Transfer the sprouts to the air fryer basket and season with the salt and pepper. Air fry for 10 to 12 minutes, until they're tender but not mushy.

SPRINKLE the Parmesan over the brussels sprouts and continue cooking for 1 to 2 minutes, until the cheese has melted. Serve warm.

Stuffed Baby Bella Mushrooms

Tender, meaty baby bella mushrooms are the perfect vehicle for delivering a prosciutto-studded, garlic-infused cream cheese filling. Serve these as an appetizer or alongside your favorite meal.

Serves 4

---

16 ounces baby bella mushrooms (about 14 to 20 mushrooms)

8 ounces plain cream cheese, softened

½ cup shredded or torn mozzarella

¼ cup shredded or grated Parmesan

2 slices prosciutto, finely chopped or shredded

¼ cup sundried tomatoes, not packed in oil, finely chopped

¼ cup Italian-seasoned bread crumbs

2 tablespoons finely chopped shallots

1 teaspoon minced garlic (about 2 medium cloves)

REMOVE the stems from the mushrooms and discard. Give the mushrooms a quick rinse and pat them dry. Set aside.

IN a large bowl, combine the cream cheese with the mozzarella and Parmesan. Mix well. Stir in the prosciutto, sundried tomatoes, bread crumbs, shallots, and garlic until the mixture is evenly combined.

FILL each mushroom cap with the filling. Arrange the mushrooms in the air fryer basket in a single layer, working in batches if necessary. Air fry at 400°F for 5 to 7 minutes, until the mushrooms are tender and the cheese has melted. Serve immediately.

Roasted Butternut Squash

While we were a little caught off guard that such a simple dish could be such a bit hit among our followers, it's for good reason: It takes virtually no time to prepare, and you get perfectly tender, caramelized squash every time. It's the ideal sweet-savory side that pairs well with just about any entrée.

Serves 4

---

1 (2-pound) butternut squash

1 tablespoon extra-virgin olive oil

2 teaspoons minced garlic or 1 teaspoon garlic powder

½ teaspoon sea salt, plus more as needed

¼ teaspoon ground black pepper, plus more as needed

Fresh parsley leaves (optional)

USING a sharp vegetable peeler, peel away the squash skin and discard. Use a large, sharp knife to cut the squash lengthwise into halves, then use a spoon to scoop out and discard the seeds. Cut the squash into 1-inch cubes.

IN a medium bowl, combine the squash with the oil, garlic, salt, and pepper. Toss to coat the squash well.

ARRANGE the squash in a single layer in the air fryer basket. You may need to do this in batches, as piling too much squash in the basket at one time will cause the squash to steam and will keep it from browning. Air fry at 400°F for 16 to 18 minutes, removing and shaking the basket halfway through the cooking process, and cooking until the squash is tender.

SEASON the squash with additional salt and pepper, if needed, and garnish with parsley, if desired.

Smoky Bacon and Three-Bean Casserole

For this updated version of baked beans, we've taken the same hearty foundation with a slightly sweet kick and added all the good things: bacon, ground beef, and cheese. Plus, we've done away with about three-quarters of the cook time that would normally be required. We love serving this dish at BBQs and potlucks, or next to a simple main for dinner.

Serves 4

6 slices of bacon	1 cup shredded mild or medium Cheddar
1 pound ground beef	1 small yellow onion, diced (about ½ cup)
1 (16-ounce) can butter beans, drained	¼ cup ketchup
1 (15.25-ounce) can lima beans, drained	¼ cup packed brown sugar
1 (11-ounce) can pork and beans	1 teaspoon Worcestershire sauce

ARRANGE the bacon in the air fryer basket in a single layer. Air fry at 400°F for 10 to 12 minutes, until crispy. Transfer to a paper towel–lined plate to cool. Break up the bacon into crumbles and set aside.

WHILE the bacon cooks, brown the beef. In a large skillet over medium heat, cook the beef, breaking it up with a spoon or spatula, until it is no longer pink, about 5 minutes.

IN a large bowl, combine the crumbled bacon, browned beef, butter beans, lima beans, pork and beans, Cheddar, onion, ketchup, brown sugar, and Worcestershire sauce. Mix well.

TRANSFER the mixture to an 8-inch round casserole or baking dish (glass or silicone) and place the dish in the air fryer basket. Air fry at 350°F for 8 to 10 minutes, stirring about halfway through, until the beans are softened. Serve warm.

Scalloped Red Potatoes

We've taken one of the most popular potato side dishes there is and given it an air fryer make-over. You still get that satisfying combination of crisped potato slices and cheesy goodness, but now you can whip this up in a fraction of the time it would take to bake and with a guarantee that your potatoes will be perfectly cooked. With very little effort, this is also a beautiful dish to put out on a holiday table.

Serves 4

½ cup shredded medium Cheddar

½ cup shredded Gruyère

½ cup shredded or grated Parmesan

¼ cup finely chopped white or yellow onion

1 teaspoon minced garlic (about 2 medium cloves)

½ teaspoon sea salt

¼ teaspoon ground black pepper

6 small red potatoes (see Note)

Avocado or olive oil cooking spray

1 cup heavy cream

IN a medium bowl, combine the Cheddar, Gruyère, Parmesan, onion, garlic, salt, and pepper. Mix well and set aside.

RINSE the potatoes and pat dry. Using a mandoline slicer or a sharp knife, thinly slice the potatoes. The slices should be so thin that they're almost translucent.

LIGHTLY spray the bottom of an 8-inch cake pan or baking dish. Arrange a layer of the potato slices, about half of the slices, over the bottom of the pan. Cover with half of the cheese mixture. Repeat with another layer of the potato slices and the remaining cheese mixture. Pour the cream over the entire dish.

AIR fry at 350°F for 13 to 15 minutes, stirring about halfway through, until the cheese has completely melted and the potato slices are tender.

NOTE: *If you are using larger potatoes, use 2 instead of 6. You want about 1½ cups of potato slices.*

Green Bean Casserole

This is one of those great all-purpose sides that can be served just as easily alongside a main on a Tuesday as it could be part of a special holiday spread. What makes it particularly great—aside from a generous portion of crispy fried onions—is that you don't need to take up valuable prep time or oven space to get it on the table.

Serves 6

---

1 (10.5-ounce) can condensed cream of mushroom soup

½ cup whole milk

½ teaspoon sea salt

½ teaspoon garlic powder

½ teaspoon ground black pepper

2 (14.5-ounce) cans green beans, drained (see Note)

1½ cups store-bought crispy fried onions

IN a medium bowl, stir together the soup, milk, salt, garlic powder, and pepper. Mix in the green beans and ¾ cup of the onions.

TRANSFER the mixture to an 8-inch round casserole or baking dish (glass or silicone). Air fry at 350°F for 10 to 12 minutes, stirring about halfway through. The casserole should be heated through. Top the casserole with the remaining ¾ cup onions and cook for another 1 to 2 minutes, until the onions are crispy.

NOTE: *You could also use fresh green beans, if you prefer. Trim 4 cups of green beans and bring a large pot of salted water to a boil. Boil the green beans for 2 to 3 minutes, until bright green and tender but not soft. Immediately transfer the green beans to a bowl of ice water and let them cool completely. Once they've been drained and blotted dry, they're ready to use!*

Lobster Mac 'n' Cheese

As two air fryer trailblazers, we've made it our mission to break common cooking misconceptions. Buckle up because we're about to throw another one your way: Cooking lobster doesn't have to be fussy, difficult, or even all that fancy, although we think adding lobster to just about anything makes it feel dressed up. This dish is the perfect mash-up of classy and casual, is essentially hands-off, and makes any meal feel special.

Serves 4

3½ cups elbow macaroni cooked according to the package instructions

1½ cups shredded sharp Cheddar

1½ cups shredded Monterey Jack

½ cup shredded mozzarella

1 large egg, beaten

½ teaspoon sea salt

½ teaspoon ground black pepper

¾ cup heavy cream

1 cup cooked lobster meat (see Note)

½ cup Italian cheese blend

Chopped fresh parsley leaves, for serving

PREHEAT the air fryer to 370°F.

IN a medium bowl, combine the cooked pasta, Cheddar, Monterey Jack, mozzarella, egg, salt, and pepper. Mix until well combined, then stir in the cream. Transfer the mixture to an 8-inch round casserole or baking dish (glass or silicone). Air fry for 8 to 10 minutes, stirring once or twice while cooking, until the cheese has melted.

OPEN the air fryer basket and stir in the lobster meat. Top the mixture with the Italian cheese blend and cook for another 3 to 5 minutes, until the top is golden brown.

ALLOW the macaroni to cool and thicken slightly, then sprinkle with parsley and serve.

NOTE: *You can use our Lobster Tails recipe on page 164 to cook the lobster meat, or you can buy canned or precooked lobster.*

Desserts

10

We like to think of this as the chapter that started it all. When Rebecca pulled out that "miracle" cheesecake from the air fryer with a perfectly set center, we knew that we had cracked the code of how to cook (and bake) at home. Using our air fryers to churn out moist cakes, silky crème brûlées, and soft, chewy cookies was just one more way to harness the power of this genius gadget while also giving us the inspiration to help millions of people get dinner AND dessert on the table in a lot less time and with less effort. We like to say that the time you'd normally spend in the kitchen making a meal is now time that you can use doing something you love with people you love, and the same goes for these recipes.

Crème Brûlée

Where do we even begin with this one? Between the assumption that you need a culinary school degree to make it and a French degree to spell it, crème brûlée seems like one of those way-too-fussy desserts to mess around with at home. But we assure you that if you're willing to follow the (very simple) steps, you'll be rewarded with the most luscious dessert we've ever come up with. You could even make these in advance and keep them in the fridge if you're having company over and want to check things off your to-do list. Add a quick trip under the broiler or a kitchen torch for that signature caramelized sugar topping and a sprinkling of fresh berries, and you're in business.

Serves 4

6 large egg yolks

⅓ cup granulated sugar, plus more for serving

2 cups heavy cream

1 teaspoon vanilla extract

¼ teaspoon ground cinnamon (optional)

Fresh berries, for serving

IN a medium bowl, whisk together the egg yolks and sugar. Continue whisking until they are well combined and a nice yellow/orange color, 2 to 3 minutes. Set aside.

IN a small saucepan over low heat, whisk together the cream, vanilla, and cinnamon (if using). Continue whisking as the mixture begins to gently simmer, then continue whisking for about another 30 seconds. Remove the pot from the heat.

WHILE whisking continuously, gradually pour the cream mixture into the egg yolks. Continue whisking until the mixture is well incorporated.

PREHEAT the air fryer at 350°F. Divide the mixture between four 4-ounce ramekins. They should be about three-quarters full. Place the ramekins in the air fryer basket and air fry for 6 to 8 minutes, until the mixture is bubbly and still slightly jiggly (it will firm up as it cools).

ALLOW the crème brûlée to cool before topping with a sprinkling of sugar (about 1 tablespoon per ramekin). You could also transfer them to the fridge to chill for at least 1 hour or up to overnight. When ready to serve, use a kitchen torch or oven broiler to caramelize the sugar until bubbling and browned. Garnish with berries and serve warm or cold.

Chocolate Bundt Cake with Chocolate Glaze

We love seeing the look on someone's face when we tell them that a baked good we're serving is fresh out of the *air fryer*. Most people don't picture dense, moist chocolate cake when they think of using this appliance, and they certainly don't expect to hear how quickly it goes from batter to Bundt. This is the perfect, simple recipe to bring to parties, to whip up for an easy weeknight dessert, or to make for no reason at all—'cause no one should need an excuse for chocolate cake.

Makes 1 (8-inch) cake

FOR THE CAKE

½ cup (8 tablespoons) unsalted butter, plus more for greasing

1 cup all-purpose flour

½ cup cocoa powder

1 teaspoon baking powder

4 ounces plain cream cheese

¾ cup granulated sugar

2 large eggs

2 teaspoons vanilla extract

FOR THE GLAZE

3 ounces unsweetened chocolate

2 tablespoons unsalted butter

1 cup powdered sugar

2 tablespoons whole milk

MAKE the cake: Grease a 7-inch Bundt pan with butter and set aside.

IN a medium bowl, whisk together the flour, cocoa powder, and baking powder. Set aside.

IN another medium bowl, combine the butter, cream cheese, and sugar. Use a hand mixer to blend until the ingredients are completely combined and creamy, about 2 minutes. (You could also do this by hand with a wooden spoon or in the bowl of a stand mixer fitted with the paddle attachment.) Beat in the eggs and vanilla and blend until mixed well.

ADD the flour mixture into the butter and sugar mixture and slowly combine until mixed well. Pour the batter into the prepared Bundt cake pan and carefully place the pan in the air fryer.

(recipe continues)

COOK at 350°F for 15 to 18 minutes, until a knife inserted in the center comes out clean. Add additional increments of 1 minute if needed. Remove the basket from the air fryer and allow the cake to cool in the pan for 2 minutes, then transfer the Bundt cake pan from the air fryer basket and allow the cake to cool completely.

MAKE the glaze: In a small saucepan over medium-low heat, melt together the chocolate and butter while continuously stirring. Remove the pot from the heat and whisk in the powdered sugar and milk until the glaze is smooth.

CAREFULLY flip the Bundt cake onto a serving dish, drizzle over the glaze, then slice and serve.

Apple Empanadas

Empanadas are a traditional Spanish treat that is similar to what we'd call a turnover—it has a flaky, golden outside and filling that's sometimes sweet, sometimes savory, but always delicious. We happen to love the story of how apple empanadas came about, which was the result of one forward-thinking cook taking their leftover dough and filling it with apples and spices. For this version, we've gone with an apple pie–like mixture made even more decadent with the addition of caramel. Both the dough and the filling come together quickly, which you'd never guess if you were served one of these fresh out of the air fryer.

Makes 6 empanadas

FOR THE DOUGH

½ cup (8 tablespoons) unsalted butter

4 ounces plain cream cheese

1 cup all-purpose flour, plus more for dusting

1 tablespoon granulated sugar

½ teaspoon vanilla extract

½ teaspoon sea salt

FOR THE FILLING

2 medium Granny Smith apples

¼ cup (4 tablespoons) unsalted butter, softened or melted

¼ cup granulated sugar

2 tablespoons packed brown sugar

2 tablespoons caramel sauce

1 tablespoon cornstarch

1 teaspoon ground cinnamon

FOR THE TOPPING

2 tablespoons unsalted butter, melted

1 tablespoon granulated sugar

1 teaspoon ground cinnamon

MAKE the dough: In a large bowl, use a fork or hand mixer to beat together the butter and cream cheese until smooth and creamy. (Alternatively, you could do this in the bowl of a stand mixer fitted with the paddle attachment.) Add the flour, sugar, vanilla, and salt and mix on medium speed until the dough forms a ball. Cover the bowl with plastic wrap and refrigerate the dough for at least 1 hour, until firm.

MAKE the filling: Peel and core the apples, then cut them into thin slices or dice them into bite-sized pieces. Add the apples to a medium bowl and stir in the butter, granulated sugar, brown sugar, caramel sauce, cornstarch, and cinnamon so the apples are well coated.

(recipe continues)

TURN out the dough onto a lightly floured work surface. Use a rolling pin to roll the dough to ⅛-inch thickness. Cut the dough into 6-inch circles. (A small bowl works well here as a template, or a pastry crimper.) Place 1 heaping tablespoon of filling in the center of each circle. Lightly brush the edges of the dough with water, then fold the circle in half over the filling. Pinch or crimp the edges together with a fork.

MAKE the topping: In a small bowl, whisk together the melted butter, sugar, and cinnamon. Brush the mixture over the top of each empanada.

ARRANGE the empanadas in a single layer in the air fryer basket and air fry at 350°F for 13 to 15 minutes, until the dough is golden brown.

Chocolate Peanut Butter Cake Mix Cookies

As if learning how to bake in the air fryer were not a great enough hack, we also figured out how to make the chewiest, fluffiest cookies with no more ingredients than you can count on one hand. The secret is using chocolate cake mix, then lacing it with creamy peanut butter and peanut butter chocolate chips. It's pretty much guaranteed gooey, decadent baking success.

Makes 24 to 30 cookies

---

1 (15.25-ounce) box chocolate cake mix

⅓ cup vegetable oil

2 large eggs

¼ cup creamy peanut butter

1 cup peanut butter chips

LINE the air fryer basket with air fryer parchment paper and set aside.

IN a large bowl, combine the cake mix, oil, eggs, and peanut butter. Mix until the ingredients are well combined and form a thick dough. Fold in the peanut butter chips until evenly distributed.

USE a 1-inch scoop or tablespoon to drop balls of dough into the prepared air fryer basket. Be sure to leave at least 1 inch between each piece of dough to allow room for the cookies to spread. You may need to cook them in batches.

AIR fry at 350°F for 6 to 7 minutes, until the cookies are golden on top. Allow the cookies to set for 1 to 2 minutes before carefully transferring them to a cooling rack to continue cooling.

STORE the fully cooled cookies in an airtight container at room temperature for up to 1 week.

Kitchen Sink Cookies

We can't decide what we like best—that this is a one-bowl recipe, that we can have warm, fresh-baked cookies in 15 minutes from start to finish, or that these cookies are a combo of *all* the mix-ins. They are a chunky, sweet-salty mash-up that tastes pretty darn perfect.

Makes 8 cookies

---

1 cup granulated sugar

½ cup (8 tablespoons) unsalted butter, softened

2 large eggs

1 teaspoon vanilla extract

1 cup all-purpose flour

½ teaspoon baking powder

½ teaspoon sea salt

½ teaspoon ground cinnamon

¼ teaspoon baking soda

1½ cups rolled oats

⅓ cup raisins

⅓ cup milk or semisweet chocolate chips

½ cup chopped pretzels

LINE the air fryer basket with air fryer parchment paper and set aside.

IN a large bowl with a hand mixer or whisk, beat together the sugar and butter until well mixed. Add the eggs and vanilla and continue beating until the mixture gets light and fluffy.

ADD the flour, baking powder, salt, cinnamon, and baking soda. Mix until well combined.

ADD the oats, raisins, chocolate chips, and pretzels and use a wooden spoon to gently fold them in until well incorporated.

USE an ice cream scoop or a large spoon to portion the dough into 8 even pieces. Arrange the pieces in the air fryer, leaving about 1 inch between them so they have room to spread. You may need to cook them in batches.

AIR fry at 300°F for 5 to 6 minutes, until the cookies are golden brown. Let the cookies rest for 1 to 2 minutes before transferring them to a cooling rack to cool completely. Store the cooled cookies in an airtight container at room temperature for up to 3 days.

NOTE: *To freeze the dough, portion out the cookies and arrange them on a baking sheet. Allow the cookies to freeze for about 1 hour before transferring them to a freezer-safe container. You can bake the cookies from frozen, but they may need a slightly longer cook time.*

Coconut Macaroons

Our favorite thing about these dense, chewy "cookies"—aside from the deep coconut flavor—is telling anyone who asks for the recipe (which is just about everyone) how easy it is to make them. We think just about anyone can handle one bowl, four ingredients, and less than 10 minutes of cook time; especially if it means getting such a sweet reward.

Makes about 24 macaroons

1 (14-ounce) bag sweetened coconut flakes

1 cup sweetened condensed milk

1 teaspoon vanilla or almond extract

¼ teaspoon sea salt

LINE the air fryer basket with air fryer parchment paper and set aside.

IN a medium bowl, combine the coconut flakes, condensed milk, vanilla or almond extract, and salt. Mix well.

USE a teaspoon or small scoop to portion the mixture onto the prepared air fryer basket, leaving ½ inch between cookies. You may need to cook these in batches.

AIR fry at 300°F for 5 to 7 minutes, until the coconut is golden brown. Allow the macaroons to cool slightly before carefully removing them from the basket.

STORE fully cooled macaroons in an airtight container at room temperature for up to 5 days.

Oatmeal-Raisin Cookies

This cookie keeps things classic with that familiar sweet-salty combination of oats and raisins. You can enjoy these all in one go, or you could do your future self a favor and freeze the portioned dough so you can bake off a cookie or two whenever the mood strikes.

Makes 8 cookies

1 cup granulated sugar	½ teaspoon baking powder
½ cup (8 tablespoons) unsalted butter, softened	½ teaspoon sea salt
2 large eggs	½ teaspoon cinnamon
1 teaspoon vanilla extract	¼ teaspoon baking soda
1 cup all-purpose flour	1½ cups rolled oats
	1 cup raisins

LINE the air fryer basket with air fryer parchment paper and set aside.

IN a large bowl with a hand mixer or whisk, beat together the sugar and butter until well mixed. Add the eggs and vanilla and continue beating until the mixture gets light and fluffy.

ADD the flour, baking powder, salt, cinnamon, and baking soda. Mix until well combined.

ADD the oats and raisins, and use a wooden spoon to gently fold them in until well incorporated.

USE an ice cream scoop or a large spoon to portion the dough into 8 even pieces. Freeze the dough at this point, or arrange the pieces in the air fryer, leaving about 1 inch between them so they have room to spread. You may need to cook these in batches.

AIR fry at 300°F for 5 to 6 minutes, until the cookies are golden brown. Let the cookies rest for 1 to 2 minutes before transferring them to a cooling rack to cool completely. Store the cooled cookies in an airtight container at room temperature for up to 3 days.

NOTE: *To freeze the dough, portion out the cookies and arrange them on a baking sheet. Allow the cookies to freeze for about 1 hour before transferring them to a freezer-safe container. You can bake the cookies from frozen, but they may need a slightly longer cook time.*

Brownie Baked Alaska

Traditionally, a baked Alaska would be a big, fancy affair with a cake that's been layered with ice cream and coated with browned meringue. Well, we are all for tradition, and all for cake, ice cream, and meringue, but not so much for big and fancy. Luckily, you can get the same effect with store-bought brownie mix, a few scoops of ice cream, and a simple meringue. And instead of needing a kitchen blowtorch to get that nice, golden meringue topping, you can use—you guessed it—your air fryer!

Serves 4

---

4 store-bought brownies

1 pint of your favorite ice cream (baked Alaska is traditionally made with Neapolitan)

2 large egg whites

¼ cup granulated sugar

1 teaspoon cream of tartar

CUT the brownies into four 3 × 3-inch squares. You could also cut them into circles that will fit in the bottom of your 4-inch ramekins.

IF you are using ramekins, place the brownies at the bottom and top with a scoop of the ice cream. Otherwise, arrange the brownies on a small baking sheet and top with a scoop of ice cream. Place the brownies and ice cream in the freezer for 15 to 30 minutes, until the ice cream is very firm.

IN a medium bowl, use a hand mixer to beat the egg whites until soft, glossy peaks form, about 2 minutes. (Alternatively, you could do this in a stand mixer fitted with the whisk attachment.) While continuing to mix, slowly add the sugar and cream of tartar. Continue mixing until glossy, stiff peaks form and the mixture thickens, 3 to 5 minutes.

IF you are not using ramekins, line the air fryer basket with air fryer parchment paper. Arrange the brownies and ice cream on top in a single layer. Use a spatula or wooden spoon to spread swirls of meringue to completely coat the ice cream and brownie on all sides. If you are using ramekins, cover the tops of each with the meringue.

AIR fry at 400°F for 3 to 5 minutes, until the meringue is golden brown and firm. Serve immediately, or freeze for up to 5 days. The meringue may soften, but the dessert will still be delicious.

Cherry Crisp

Everyone should have a classic crisp recipe in their repertoire, especially a cherry version for the summer. Instead of using a traditional baking dish, we love making this in individual ramekins, so everyone gets their own personal portion. Every scoop is the perfect combination of juicy, tart filling and a brown sugar oat crumble topping.

Serves 4

FOR THE FILLING

2 cups fresh or frozen cherries, pitted and halved

1 tablespoon granulated sugar

1 teaspoon cornstarch

1 teaspoon vanilla extract

FOR THE TOPPING

¼ cup (4 tablespoons) unsalted butter, melted

½ cup packed brown sugar

½ cup old-fashioned oats

¼ cup all-purpose flour

½ teaspoon ground cinnamon

Avocado or olive oil cooking spray

MAKE the filling: In a medium bowl, combine the cherries, sugar, cornstarch, and vanilla. Stir to mix well. Set aside.

MAKE the topping: In a separate medium bowl, combine the melted butter, brown sugar, oats, flour, and cinnamon. Stir until the mixture is crumbly in consistency. Set aside.

LIGHTLY coat 4 ramekins with the cooking spray, then equally divide the cherry filling between the ramekins. Sprinkle the topping over the filling, but without completely covering the cherries.

ARRANGE the ramekins in the air fryer basket and air fry at 350°F for 8 to 10 minutes, until the topping is golden brown and crisp, and the cherry filling is bubbling.

Classic Chocolate Cupcakes

A one-bowl cupcake recipe that bakes up in 10 minutes and delivers rich, chocolatey flavor? You bet. This recipe is particularly fun for getting the kids involved—and handy for those moments when you have that special occasion/potluck/bake sale and want to serve something homemade but don't have all afternoon to bake.

Makes 16 cupcakes

1½ cups all-purpose flour

1 cup granulated sugar

⅓ cup cocoa powder

1 teaspoon baking soda

½ teaspoon sea salt

1 cup whole milk

¼ cup vegetable oil

1 large egg

1 tablespoon white vinegar

1 (16-ounce) container store-bought frosting

IN a large bowl with a hand mixer or whisk, or in the bowl of a stand mixer fitted with the paddle attachment, combine the flour, sugar, cocoa powder, baking soda, and salt. Mix well. Add the milk, oil, egg, and vinegar. Beat together on medium speed until the batter is smooth, scraping the sides of the bowl to incorporate all of the ingredients.

EVENLY divide the batter between 16 silicone muffin cups, making sure none are more than three-quarters full (see Note). Carefully transfer the muffin cups to the air fryer basket and air fry at 300°F for 10 to 12 minutes, until a toothpick inserted in the center of a cupcake comes out clean. You may need to do this in batches.

ALLOW the cupcakes to cool completely before frosting as desired.

NOTE: *If you divide the batter between fewer muffin cups, just be sure to not fill them more than three-quarters full. Otherwise, the fan from the air fryer may "lift" the batter and your cupcakes will be misshapen.*

Deep-Dish Brownies

We've always embraced the efficiency of store-bought shortcuts, whether it's pie crust, pizza dough, or cake mix. But sometimes from-scratch is worth it, especially when you dig into your own single serving of rich, dense brownie. What's even sweeter is that these only call for a short list of ingredients that you most likely already have in the kitchen, and by making them in ramekins, there's barely any cleanup required. (Namely because everyone tends to lick their ramekin clean!)

Makes 4 brownies

Avocado or olive oil cooking spray

½ cup (8 tablespoons) unsalted butter, at room temperature

¾ cup granulated sugar

1 teaspoon vanilla extract

2 large eggs

½ cup all-purpose flour

¼ cup cocoa powder

½ teaspoon baking powder

¼ teaspoon sea salt

1 cup mini semisweet chocolate chips

LIGHTLY coat four 3-inch ramekins with the cooking spray and set aside.

IN the bowl of a stand mixer fitted with the paddle attachment or in a large bowl with a hand mixer or spoon, use medium/medium-high speed to beat together the butter, sugar, and vanilla until smooth and creamy. Add the eggs and continue mixing until well combined. Reduce the speed to low/medium and add the flour, cocoa powder, baking powder, and salt. Mix until a smooth batter forms. Use a spoon or spatula to fold in the chocolate chips until evenly distributed.

EVENLY divide the batter between the ramekins (about ⅔ cup batter per ramekin) and place them in the air fryer basket. Air fry at 300°F for 22 to 24 minutes, until firm.

Old-Fashioned Oatmeal Cake

Oats are another great baking secret weapon because of how they give cakes nice, dense body and subtle oatmeal flavor. Combined with brown sugar and nutmeg plus a golden coconut topping, it's like enjoying a warm bowl of oats on a cold winter morning—cozy and satisfying.

Makes 1 (8-inch) cake

FOR THE CAKE

Avocado or olive oil cooking spray

¾ cup boiling water

½ cup quick or old-fashioned oats

¼ cup (4 tablespoons) unsalted butter

½ cup packed brown sugar

½ cup granulated sugar

1 large egg

¾ cup plus 2 tablespoons all-purpose flour

½ teaspoon ground cinnamon

½ teaspoon baking soda

¼ teaspoon baking powder

¼ teaspoon sea salt

¼ teaspoon ground nutmeg

FOR THE COCONUT TOPPING

1 cup sweetened shredded coconut

⅔ cup packed brown sugar

¼ cup (4 tablespoons) unsalted butter, melted

¼ cup slivered almonds (optional)

3 tablespoons whole milk

1 teaspoon vanilla extract

MAKE the cake: Line an 8-inch cake pan with air fryer parchment paper and lightly coat with cooking spray. Set aside.

IN a medium bowl, combine the boiling water and oats and let them soak for 10 minutes.

MEANWHILE, in the bowl of a stand mixer fitted with the paddle attachment or in a large bowl with a hand mixer or spoon, beat together the butter, brown sugar, and granulated sugar on medium speed until it resembles wet sand. Add the egg and continue mixing for 30 seconds, until well incorporated.

ADD the flour, cinnamon, baking soda, baking powder, salt, and nutmeg and mix until well combined. Add the oatmeal and mix until a thick batter forms, scraping down the sides of the bowl as needed.

POUR the batter into the prepared pan and air fry at 300°F for 23 to 25 minutes, until a toothpick inserted in the center of the cake comes out clean.

(recipe continues)

WHILE the cake bakes, make the coconut topping (see Note): In a medium bowl, stir together the coconut, brown sugar, butter, almonds (if using), milk, and vanilla. When the cake is done baking, evenly spread the topping over the cake and air fry at 350°F for 5 to 8 minutes, until the top is golden brown.

NOTE: *If you don't have time to add the topping or prefer to skip it for any reason, you can easily substitute it with a frosting of your choice.*

Creamy Peanut Butter Cake

Everyone needs a recipe for a celebration cake, even if the reason for celebrating is "just be-cause." This recipe yields a decadently rich, moist, peanut buttery cake with a chocolate frost-ing that will make you want to come up with new special occasions to commemorate. And for extra-extra-special occasions, you can double this recipe to make a double-layer cake.

Makes 1 (8-inch) cake

Avocado or olive oil cooking spray	⅓ cup granulated sugar
1 cup all-purpose flour	⅓ cup packed brown sugar
1 teaspoon baking soda	1 large egg
Pinch of sea salt	1 teaspoon vanilla extract
½ cup peanut butter (creamy or crunchy)	¾ cup whole milk
⅓ cup vegetable oil	1 (16-ounce) container chocolate frosting

---

LINE an 8-inch cake pan with air fryer parchment paper and lightly coat the sides with cooking spray. Set aside.

IN a medium bowl, whisk together the flour, baking soda, and salt. Set aside.

IN the bowl of a stand mixer fitted with the paddle attachment or in a large bowl with a hand mixer or spoon, beat together the peanut butter, oil, granulated sug-ar, and brown sugar on medium speed until smooth and creamy. Add the egg and vanilla and mix until combined. While continuing to mix, slowly add the milk and mix until smooth. Still mixing, slowly add the flour mixture until well com-bined.

POUR the batter into the prepared pan and air fry at 320°F for 10 minutes. Care-fully cover the cake with foil and air fry for an additional 15 to 20 minutes, until a toothpick inserted in the center of the cake comes out clean.

ALLOW the cake to cool in the pan for about 5 minutes, then carefully transfer the cake to a cooling rack to cool completely. Top with the chocolate frosting.

NOTE: *The top of the cake may have a swirl from the fan in the air fryer. This is normal and can be trimmed down before frosting. If desired, use a large serrated knife to evenly cut across the very top of the cake to create a more even surface before frosting. To make a two-layer cake, you can double the cake and frosting recipe and stack the two cakes with a layer of frosting between them.*

Apple Dumplings

Even though the word *dumplings* calls to mind delicious, doughy, gooey, fresh-from-the-oven treats your grandmother might have made you, it also sounds like . . . a lot of work. But by wrapping store-bought dough around apple slices and brushing them with a cinnamon-sugar butter, you can have these mini apple pie–like dumplings in under 15 minutes. Better yet? Serve them warm with a scoop of vanilla ice cream.

Serves 4

2 Granny Smith apples

2 (8-ounce) cans crescent dough, separated into triangles

1 cup packed brown sugar

¾ cup (12 tablespoons) unsalted butter, plus more for greasing

1½ teaspoons ground cinnamon

1 teaspoon vanilla extract

Pinch of kosher salt

Vanilla ice cream, for serving

PREHEAT the air fryer to 350°F.

PEEL and core the apples, then slice them each into eighths. Lay the pieces of dough on a clean work surface. Lay an apple slice horizontally at the wide end of one of the triangles, then roll up the dough toward the tip of the triangle. Repeat with the remaining slices of apple. Arrange the dumplings in the air fryer basket in a single layer and set aside.

IN a small saucepan over medium heat, combine the brown sugar, butter, cinnamon, vanilla, and salt. Stir as the butter melts completely, then pour the mixture over the dumplings.

AIR fry the dumplings for 5 to 7 minutes, until golden brown. Serve warm with vanilla ice cream.

Rebecca's Miracle Cheesecake

This is the recipe that started it all! As an air fryer newbie, Rebecca wanted to see what this gadget could really do, so she threw at it one of the more finicky baking recipes she had in her repertoire: a cheesecake. If there's too big of a swing in temperatures, a draft in the oven, or you just look at it the wrong way, a cheesecake will crack right down the middle. Will it still be delicious? Most definitely. But if you're going to put the time and effort into making a perfectly silky, creamy cheesecake, you want a perfectly smooth top. Well, Rebecca put it to the test in the air fryer, and sure enough—after a few tries—out came a picture-perfect cheesecake. It made us wonder, *What else can this baby do?* And hundreds of recipes later, the rest is history.

While this cake might feel like it requires a special occasion, we insist that there's no reason *not* to make it whenever the mood strikes. Top it off with cherry pie filling and toast to your air fryer.

Makes 1 (7-inch) cake

Avocado or olive oil cooking spray

1½ cups graham crackers (12 whole graham crackers)

½ cup (8 tablespoons) salted butter, melted

24 ounces plain cream cheese, at room temperature

1 (14-ounce) can sweetened condensed milk

2 large eggs

1 teaspoon vanilla extract

1 (21-ounce) can cherry pie filling

LINE the bottom and sides of a 7-inch (see Note) springform pan with air frying parchment paper and lightly coat with cooking spray. (It's crucial that you spray the sides well; this will help you remove the cheesecake after it bakes.)

IN a food processor, pulse the graham crackers until they are finely ground. Transfer them to a small bowl. Stir the butter into the ground graham crackers until fully combined. Press the mixture into the bottom of the prepared pan, using a spoon to pack it down firmly. Set aside.

(recipe continues)

IN the bowl of a stand mixer fitted with the paddle attachment or in a large bowl with a hand mixer on medium speed, beat the cream cheese until smooth, 2 to 3 minutes. Add the condensed milk, eggs, and vanilla and continue blending until the mixture is completely smooth, about 2 minutes.

POUR the cream cheese mixture into the prepared pan over the graham cracker crust. It will fill the pan almost completely. Carefully transfer the pan to the air fryer basket and air fry at 300°F for 20 to 22 minutes, until the center is no longer jiggling. (It will wiggle, but it won't be a wet jiggle.) If needed, continue adding 2-minute increments to the cook time at 300°F until the center is perfect.

ALLOW the cake to cool slightly before carefully removing the pan from the basket and transferring it to the refrigerator. Let the cake chill for 6 to 8 hours or up to overnight.

WHEN the cake has set, remove the sides of the pan and transfer the cake to a serving platter. Top with the cherry pie filling, slice, and serve.

STORE any leftovers in an airtight container in the refrigerator for up to 3 days.

NOTE: *If necessary, you can use an 8-inch springform pan for this recipe. You'll need to increase the graham crackers to 2 cups to cover the bottom. Bake at 300°F for 15 minutes, adding 2-minute increments as needed until the middle is set.*

Lemon Pudding Cake

We've taken a classic Bundt cake and given it a pop of bright lemony flavor. Adding lemon pudding mix to the batter not only gives you that great taste, it also lends this cake a moist, tender crumb that makes it so much more special. This would be right at home as part of a polished brunch spread, on a barbecue dessert table, or even served for breakfast.

Serves 4 to 6

Avocado or olive oil cooking spray

½ cup (8 tablespoons) unsalted butter, at room temperature

4 ounces plain cream cheese, at room temperature

¾ cup granulated sugar

2 large eggs

1 teaspoon lemon extract

1 cup all-purpose flour

1 teaspoon baking powder

1 (3.4-ounce) box lemon pudding mix

1 (16-ounce) container white, vanilla, or lemon frosting (optional)

LIGHTLY coat the Bundt pan with the cooking spray and set aside.

IN the bowl of a stand mixer fitted with the paddle attachment or in a large bowl with a hand mixer or spoon, beat together the butter, cream cheese, and sugar until the batter is smooth and creamy.

ADD the eggs and lemon extract and mix until combined. While continuing to mix, slowly add the flour and baking powder until a thick batter forms. Use a spoon to stir in the lemon pudding mix.

POUR the batter into the prepared pan and air fry at 350°F for 15 to 18 minutes, until the cake is firm and golden. Allow the cake to cool in the pan for about 5 minutes before carefully turning it out onto a cooling rack. Allow the cake to cool completely before frosting, if desired.

NOTE: *You will need a 6-inch Bundt pan to make this recipe.*

Acknowledgments

We would like to thank our families, dear friends, and neighbors, who have not only supported us along the way, but have tirelessly tasted and tested our recipes. We would also like to share our deepest thanks and gratitude to:

New York Times food writer Christina Morales for sharing our story with the world.

Our HarperCollins dream team, Sarah Pelz, Emma Peters, and Alison Bloomer—you are all exceptional and we can't thank you enough for making this book a reality.

Our agent, Janis Donnaud, for making the call. Your encouragement and support has been priceless.

Rachel Holtzman for being so talented and helping us turn our words into a story.

Air Fryer Cooking Times and Temps

SEAFOOD	TEMP	TIME
Shrimp	400°F	5 minutes
Fish Fillet	400°F	10 minutes
Tuna Steak	400°F	7 to 10 minutes
Mahi-Mahi	350°F	12 minutes
Salmon	380°F	12 minutes
Scallops	400°F	5 to 7 minutes
Fish Sticks (frozen)	400°F	12 minutes
Lobster Tail	380°F	6 to 8 minutes
Crab Legs	370°F	5 to 7 minutes
VEGETABLES	TEMP	TIME
Asparagus	400°F	5 minutes
Baked Potato	400°F	40 minutes
Baked Sweet Potato	380°F	40 minutes
Baby Potatoes	400°F	15 minutes
Home Cut French Fries	380°F	14 to 16 minutes
Zucchini Sticks	400°F	12 minutes
Corn on the Cob	390°F	6 minutes
Carrots	380°F	15 minutes
Eggplant	400°F	15 minutes

BEEF	TEMP	TIME
Meatball	380°F	7 to 10 minutes
Rib Eye Steak	400°F	12 to 15 minutes
Sirloin Steak (12 oz.)	400°F	10 to 15 minutes
Beef Round Roast	390°F	45 to 55 minutes
Burgers	370°F	16 to 20 minutes
Filet Mignon	380°F	12 to 16 minutes
POULTRY	TEMP	TIME
Whole Chicken (3 lbs.)	360°F	60 to 70 minutes
Boneless Chicken Breast	360°F	19 minutes
Drumsticks	370°F	20 minutes
Thighs, Bone in	380°F	22 minutes
Thighs, Boneless	380°F	18 to 20 minutes
Wings	360° to 390°F	20 minutes
Tenders	360°F	8 to 10 minutes
Chicken Nuggets (frozen)	400°F	10 to 12 minutes
Boneless Turkey Breast	350°F	45 to 55 minutes
Cornish Game Hens	350°F	30 minutes
Duck	300°F	45 to 55 minutes
PORK	TEMP	TIME
Pork Chops	400°F	12 to 14 minutes
Pork Tenderloin	370°F	15 minutes
Bacon	400°F	5 to 7 minutes
Bacon (thick cut)	400°F	6 to 10 minutes
Pork Loin	360°F	55 minutes
Sausage	380°F	15 minutes
Ribs	380°F	30 minutes

Universal Conversion Chart

OVEN TEMPERATURE EQUIVALENTS

250°F = 120°C

275°F = 135°C

300°F = 150°C

325°F = 160°C

350°F = 180°C

375°F = 190°C

400°F = 200°C

425°F = 220°C

450°F = 230°C

475°F = 240°C

500°F = 260°C

MEASUREMENT EQUIVALENTS

Measurements should always be level unless directed otherwise.

⅛ teaspoon = 0.5 mL

¼ teaspoon = 1 mL

½ teaspoon = 2 mL

1 teaspoon = 5 mL

1 tablespoon = 3 teaspoons = ½ fluid ounce = 15 mL

2 tablespoons = ⅛ cup = 1 fluid ounce = 30 mL

4 tablespoons = ¼ cup = 2 fluid ounces = 60 mL

5⅓ tablespoons = ⅓ cup = 3 fluid ounces = 80 mL

8 tablespoons = ½ cup = 4 fluid ounces = 120 mL

10⅔ tablespoons = ⅔ cup = 5 fluid ounces = 160 mL

12 tablespoons = ¾ cup = 6 fluid ounces = 180 mL

16 tablespoons = 1 cup = 8 fluid ounces = 240 mL

Index

Note: Page references in *italics* indicate photographs.

About the Authors

After years of working as a bank manager, **REBECCA ABBOTT** left the corporate world to become a high school culinary arts teacher. Rebecca realized that she loved the challenge of mastering the science of cooking, particularly baking. She eventually left teaching to spend more time with her grandchildren, but after meeting Jennifer, she returned to her passion of sharing recipes, specifically those she made in the air fryer. Rebecca and her husband are also marathon runners and have completed several half and full marathons, including the Dublin Marathon and the New York City Marathon. Rebecca and her husband currently reside in Mesa, Arizona.

JENNIFER WEST is a former medical device representative who spent over ten years working in the medical field. Meanwhile, she loved sharing her passion for cooking so much that she started posting her recipes online. It was then that she decided to retire from sales and make her hobby of cooking her new career. Jennifer loves to play tennis and pickleball, as well as travel. She and her family reside in Shreveport, Louisiana.

"*Air Fryer All Day* is filled with mouthwatering recipes and beautiful images that will make you excited to use your air fryer at every opportunity. I'm confident you'll find your new favorite meal within its pages!"
—Stephanie Keeping, blogger at *Spaceships and Laser Beams*

"Jennifer and Rebecca not only bring you tons of mouthwatering air fryer recipes to make, they guide you on selecting an air fryer, show you how to use it properly, and provide conversion charts and even a handy toast test to make sure your meals come out perfect every time. I love the variety of recipes in this book and can't wait to get cooking!"
—Amanda Formaro, blogger at *Amanda's Cookin'*

About the Authors

After years of working as a bank manager, **REBECCA ABBOTT** left the corporate world to become a high school culinary arts teacher. Rebecca realized that she loved the challenge of mastering the science of cooking, particularly baking. She eventually left teaching to spend more time with her grandchildren, but after meeting Jennifer, she returned to her passion of sharing recipes, specifically those she made in the air fryer. Rebecca and her husband are also marathon runners and have completed several half and full marathons, including the Dublin Marathon and the New York City Marathon. Rebecca and her husband currently reside in Mesa, Arizona.

JENNIFER WEST is a former medical device representative who spent over ten years working in the medical field. Meanwhile, she loved sharing her passion for cooking so much that she started posting her recipes online. It was then that she decided to retire from sales and make her hobby of cooking her new career. Jennifer loves to play tennis and pickleball, as well as travel. She and her family reside in Shreveport, Louisiana.

HarperCollins books may be purchased for educational, business, or sales promotional use. For information, please email the Special Markets Department at SPsales@harpercollins.com.

FIRST EDITION

Designed by Alison Bloomer

Food photography by Debby Wolvos except for page 61 by Jennifer West and page 213 by Rebecca Abbott
Food styling by Kimberly Bregger | Photoshoot assistant: Katie Gourdin
Lifestyle photography by Lenny Catalanotto except for page 230 by Debby Wolvos

Library of Congress Cataloging-in-Publication Data

Names: Abbott, Rebecca, author. | West, Jennifer (Co founder of Air Frying Foodie), author. | Holtzman, Rachel, author.
Title: Air fryer all day : 120 tried-and-true recipes for family-friendly comfort food / Rebecca Abbott and Jennifer West, co founders of Air Frying Foodie with Rachel Holtzman.
Description: First edition. | New York : Harvest, an imprint of William Morrow, [2023] | Includes index.
Identifiers: LCCN 2023010142 (print) | LCCN 2023010143 (ebook) | ISBN 9780063289376 (hardback) | ISBN 9780063289413 (ebook)
Subjects: LCSH: Hot air frying. | Comfort food. | LCGFT: Cookbooks.
Classification: LCC TX689 .A24 2023 (print) | LCC TX689 (ebook) | DDC 641.7/7—dc23/eng/20230310
LC record available at https://lccn.loc.gov/2023010142
LC ebook record available at https://lccn.loc.gov/2023010143

ISBN 978-0-06-328937-6

23 24 25 26 27 IMG 10 9 8 7 6 5 4 3 2 1

"*Air Fryer All Day* is filled with mouthwatering recipes and beautiful images that will make you excited to use your air fryer at every opportunity. I'm confident you'll find your new favorite meal within its pages!"
—Stephanie Keeping, blogger at *Spaceships and Laser Beams*

"Jennifer and Rebecca not only bring you tons of mouthwatering air fryer recipes to make, they guide you on selecting an air fryer, show you how to use it properly, and provide conversion charts and even a handy toast test to make sure your meals come out perfect every time. I love the variety of recipes in this book and can't wait to get cooking!"
—Amanda Formaro, blogger at *Amanda's Cookin'*